Table of Contents

Foreword

By Dr. P. Qasimah Boston, MPH, CHES

How do you know, what life is all about? Can you find it in your own world? Do you venture out to see what humanity has to offer? Perhaps exploration of examples of life and living may provide insights helpful to discovery of destiny and paths to reaching the highest level of humanity. My friend Regina had a stem cell transplant. After the transplant came GVHD - Graft versus Host Disease. Many have never heard of this. It can happen after a stem cell transplant when the new cells see the body as foreign and then attack the body. The darkness under Regina's eyes, under her armpits, under her breast and the throat and stomach problems she has are the results of the stem cell transplant she had. According to the United States National Library of Medicine, the chance of GVHD is around 30 to 40% when the cell recipient is related to the donor.

Let me share something with you. On a very special morning that was beautiful, hot and sunny, I was driven to get up early, to dress up, in my best and to walk. I did not know where the walk would take me I just knew that I was on a Spirit filled walk to find and to receive. On that day, I walked through the streets of Savannah, Georgia. During most of the walk I thought the reason was to find a job, and it was. Although many doors were closed in my face, I kept walking, kept searching -- looking for my next job. I found it. My next job was my next mission and my next blessing on my journey. My job, which was my next mission, blessing and honor was to become lifelong friends with Mrs. Regina Thompson by connecting to Spirit and being in Spirit.

The late highly regarded poet, Maya Angelou is so eloquent when she shares her writing, "A Rock, A River, A Tree." In this writing she says:

But today, the Rock cries out to us, clearly, forcefully,
Come, you may stand upon my
Back and face your distant destiny,
But seek no haven in my shadow.
I will give you no hiding place down here.
You, created only a little lower than
The angels, have crouched too long in
The bruising darkness.

On this beautiful morning in Savannah, I met a beautiful "Rock" "Angel" named, Mrs. Regina Thompson who said just this to me – "come, you may stand upon my back and face your distant destiny." While I did not know at the time I met her that she had recently received treatment for a health condition called, lymphoma or, cancer of the lymph, her existence in my life was pivotal and Spirit given. As I walked through the hot Savannah, Georgia streets, Regina called out to me as she sat in her craft shop on Abercorn Street watching me pass by and I followed the beautiful voice that did not close the door in my face, but rather opened the door on that day. Regina was diagnosed with non-Hodgkin's lymphoma in 1995. Her father was diagnosed with the same condition in the same year. Her treatment was a stem cell transplant from her brother Keith and blood transfusions from her brother Calvin. Both her brothers were perfect matches.

I am not sure how long after I met Regina that she shared with me her health experience with lymphoma, and the stand that she purposely takes to not allow lymphoma to stop her life and living or to take over her life and living. Regina did and has always amazed me with her candidness, spiritual fortitude, and her overall faith. For me, she is the healthiest person on the earth because her practice of living in Spirit and in Faith far exceeds many of the most powerful people that I know. Regina knows that her healing is in sharing her journey and experience. She knows that she has been divinely chosen to pass on her ups and downs with lymphoma, her family, her marriage, her womanhood and her inspiration.

Regina and her life is filled with human triumph, courage, devotion, passion, tears, laughter all mixed with the power of love, the power of hope, the power of faith and the power of the practice of truly taking the path to reach the highest level of humanity. Regina embraces and recognizes the divine mission she was sent here for is more than profound, it is critical and crucial for all human struggle and human challenge.

She shares her life experience with lymphoma in this book. She shares that it is a challenge, not to fight, but to bring her closer to the practice of being totally connected to Spirit and working with Spirit. Regina is it and in this riveting rendition of her true life experience, she is the practice of allowing a life experience to help us reach the highest level of humanity. – AND SO IT IS!

Preface

The purpose of this book is to share with people how my cancer diagnoses were truly both a challenge and a gift for me. Cancer was an all too familiar existence on my father's side of the family. What was apparent and puzzling growing up in my family was that being diagnosed with cancer was a shameful situation and no one was willing to talk about it.

There was however one person who was my inspiration for writing this book. Auntie (Mary Eliza) was unknowingly the catalyst in helping me decide what I needed to do to beat cancer. She was truly a champion in how she managed cancer. She made it known what she had; in fact she kept a clipping of an article explaining in detail what type of cancer she was fighting at the front door of her home. If guests had any questions she would have them read the material for understanding of the disease. Her siblings thought this was crazy, but she did not let it deter her from educating. For her education was power. She made peace with what was to come and she continued to live her life accordingly until cancer called her home to glory or as she would refer to it as "going home to be with my Lord".

I am sharing my spiritual journey with cancer to illuminate numerous obstacles which turned into life lessons. I learned how to release the obstacles in my past that were blocking my blessings. Coming from a time when children were seen and not heard, cancer allowed me the opportunity to discover my own voice. This disease gave me the strength and courage to speak up for myself. I learned to maintain serenity in the midst of adversity and chaos. This allowed me to tune out the noise and listen to my spirit allowing it to guide me on this journey. Most importantly, I learned how to open my heart to receive the love from the supporters that surrounded me and my family.

This journey forced me to peel back the layers of my life, the layers of my past, and project my existing vigor to survive. I learned just how powerful my connection was with my mind and body. I became empowered to cultivate the aspects needed to get through my cancer journey. Navigating my own life from the driver's seat gave me the awareness that the only factor I controlled was the present moment.

CANCER!

Accept,

Release,

Speak,

HEAL!!!

Chapter 1: SIGNS

I had a reoccurring dream that I was traveling in a commercial neighborhood alongside eighteen wheeler trucks and there was thick fog in the air. All of a sudden the scene changed to my mom's home. My husband David was standing by the door of the room, my aunt sitting in a chair, and Mom on the opposite side of the room. The alarming sight was the body that laid lifeless on the floor covered with a white sheet. I circled the room asking everyone what was going on, but they acted as if I was not there. There was a look of dread on David's face, while my aunt stood by very distraught. This dream transpired repeatedly for months and I could not make sense of it.

During this time, I was employed by the Department of Labor as a front desk clerk. One day a woman came in to list a job for her organization and I was extremely impressed by her demeanor and drawn in by her positive energy. Something inside me said I was going to apply for the job and that I needed to do everything I could to get the job. In preparation for the interview, I practiced techniques to impress the interviewing officials, which after hired I found was unnecessary. The job was located in the industrial area of Savannah where commercial eighteen wheeler trucks dominated the roads on my daily commute to work.

I found myself craving for positive affirmations and positive energy. The Christian bookstore became a field trip for me during most of my lunch breaks. Reading material pertaining to God's word uplifted and energized me. After attending my newly found family church for several months, I began to volunteer to host Bible study at my home occasionally. Having Gods' word around me constantly helped me gain confidence and strength in my spirit, and allowed me to deal with the unceasing stress life was throwing. My stress levels were high as a result of internalizing my feelings; therefore I began to explore ways to release stress.

The first apparent sign of change within my body occurred one day at the park. It was routine for me to go out to Lake Meyer (in Southside Savannah) to counteract stress through exercise about four to six days a week, which made it effortless to notice change within my body.

On one particular day like all others I was at the park, but only this time I found it difficult to catch my breath with each step I made around the park. I was forced to take deep breaths in an attempt to catch my breath. By the end of a mile and a half walk, I was extremely tired not to mention I was completely out of breath. I brushed it off as just having a long exhausting day at work. Soon I realized how difficult it became climbing stairs at home and the steep concrete steps that lead up to the office building where I worked. Getting through each day became harder and harder to accomplish. The ride home from work was challenging because I would drift off to sleep at stop lights. After returning from work each evening, I had very little energy remaining to do the normal routine with my children. I would go directly to bed leaving my thirteen year old to care for himself and five year old sister until my husband returned from work.

I knew I needed to drop about 15 to 20 pounds but any attempt I made to work it off was becoming almost impossible. Physical changes occurred over the next few months. I experienced frequent headaches, extreme fatigue, severe constipation, and constant perspiration.

Very little energy had to be exerted to break out into an intense moment of perspiration. Fevers would come and go causing me to sometimes miss work. Unfortunately, these symptoms became an unwelcoming part of my day to day routine. This progressed for several months before coming to the realization that I needed to figure out what was going on. The only sensible step left to take was to consult with a doctor.

My visit to the physician had an unexpected response. I anticipated the doctor to at least tell me what I was doing wrong or what I needed to do to fix the problem. Instead, he told me that I was in my early thirty's and with that a woman experiences many bodily changes during this stage of her life. He also stated that my complete blood count, which is also known as CBC red blood count was a little low and that I was anemic as well as being overweight. This made me feel that aging was the cause of all my problems and the cure was to lose a few pounds. I did not question the doctor because after all he was subject matter expert and he was "experienced" at his profession. Again, I attempted to lose a few pounds. Almost instantaneously the same things continued to occur; headaches, constant perspiration and difficulty breathing whenever I over exerted myself. I then decided to choose another doctor hoping to get diet pills to boost the weight loss which I was told the cause of my discomfort and grief derived from.

During this visit, the medical officials made me feel as though I was simply a complaining woman experiencing life changes. She performed blood work and comparable to previous results showed my red blood cell count was low enough which sparked her interest in further pursuing the root cause. With this being said I still did not receive a prescription for diet pills like I had in mind. In order to understand the cause of the low red blood count, over the next three weeks my doctor evaluated me through a series of blood tests which all yielded negative results. It was Friday before Mother's Day in 1995, when my doctor called at work requesting that I come in for additional tests. At the end of the work day all the women wished each other a wonderful Mother's Day weekend. I went home and did my best to have an enjoyable weekend.

I decided to do my best to refrain from worrying or

focusing on any medical issues. The weekend with the children was wonderful. As usual, my children and husband showered me with much love and gifts. On Sunday, which was actually Mother's Day, my family treated me to a wonderful restaurant for dinner. At dinner I noticed an overwhelming feeling of fullness just after a few bites of my meal. I told my husband that I was unable to eat much more of my dinner which we agreed was odd. We decided to take the remainder home and completely relax for the evening. As my husband and I sat in bed we talked about the great weekend that we had with the children. On a more serious note, I told my husband that I felt as though something seriously wrong was occurring with my body. He assured me that the doctor would more than likely figure out what exactly was happening with the up-coming test on Monday.

The next morning, I stumbled into the bathroom extremely tired as usual to get dressed for work and I noticed my stomach was protruding. I looked like I was five or six months pregnant. I continued to dress and my clothes were terribly snug, although I did not experience discomfort, I still believed my visit to the doctor was necessary to understand what was happening. Upon my arrival at work the first thing the secretary noticed when I walked through the door was my enlarged abdomen; she even made a wise joke, "Girl what in God's name did you and your husband do over the weekend? Regina you look like you are pregnant." My manager was not at work so I called to inform her of my situation and urgency to go see my doctor that morning. My manager shared with me her belief that an enema could cure all ailments. She suggested that I take a laxative and guaranteed my stomach would subside. I called my doctor to try to schedule an earlier appointment, but it was unsuccessful. At lunch, I decided not to wait until later and instead I went to the emergency room.

Chapter 2: CANCER

Upon my arrival to the emergency room, it just so happened that I was the only person. They processed me right away. I explained to the doctor on duty the reason for my visit and almost immediately a series of tests were performed; then I was placed in an exam room to wait for the results. Only minutes after I had gotten dressed to wait for the doctor I tuned into the Young and the Restless and at that very moment my husband walked through the door of my exam room. He explained that he called the office to see how I was feeling and the secretary told him where to find me. He expressed to me that he felt his presence was needed at the hospital. I shared with him that I was feeling uncanny and that the news from the doctor was not going to be positive. Before I could finish the sentence the emergency room attending doctor came in with an odd expression on his face. He started to explain that the protrusion in my stomach was the result of my spleen being enlarged and that the x-ray's showed that I had lymphoma. My immediate response was, "what exactly is lymphoma?" He explained that lymphoma is a form of cancer. I started asking more questions and he quickly advised me that it would be best to talk in depth with my doctor. He informed us that he had notified my general doctor and that I needed to go directly to her office.

The drive to my doctor's office only took ten minutes, but it seemed like an hour. David and I did not say anything to each other on the drive to the office. When we entered, the nurse quickly took me into a room and the doctor entered with a list of directives. I interrupted her sequence of instructions and asked was the diagnosis serious and she paused. Eventually her reply was, "Yes very serious." I then asked if I would die from this and she said again that it was very serious. She left me and my husband in the room and I turned to David I told him that I dreamed about this moment and that in my dream someone in my family became very ill and died. The doctor peered into the room and instructed me to come into her office to talk to an Oncologist via telephone. She stated he was one of the best oncologists in this area.

"My name is Dr. Badal" he said, "Regina I need for you to go back to the hospital to be admitted. Your spleen is enlarged and the slightest bump could cause it to rupture and you would only have a few minutes before needing emergency surgery as a result." I quickly explained to him that I could not do that because my children were about to get out of school and I had to pick them up and get them situated first and then I could go to the hospital. He very sternly said, "Mrs. Thompson I don't think you understand the seriousness of this situation." My response was simply, "You don't understand my children are very important to me and I need to get them taken care of first and then I will go back to the hospital."

The oncologist once again explained that any force or trauma to my stomach could cause my spleen to rupture and I would have only minutes to get to a doctor to save my life. He advised me to be very careful and as soon as I could to go directly to the hospital afterwards. I hung up from him and called my job and told the secretary that I would not be coming back to work today and that I did not know when I would return. The secretary asked what was wrong and I told her that the doctor said I had "CANCER." David and I left the doctor's office to pick up the children from school. We got the children home and I rushed straight up to my bedroom and called my friend Mandy. When she answered the phone I quickly blurted out, "Mandy", with a crackling voice, "I have cancer." She said, "Regina is that you, where is David?" At that moment I started to cry hysterically about everything that was reported earlier. Mandy with her usual calm voice asked me again where David was and told me to go down stairs to be with him and reassured me that she would be over soon.

Next, I called my mother and told her the life-changing news. My mother in turn informed me that she just found out today that my father was diagnosed with lymphoma. He was diagnosed a few months earlier and was secretly taking himself to the doctor for treatments without any family knowing about it. He began having trouble driving to the treatments which is why he needed my mother to take him now. She then put my father on the phone and his first words to me were, "Baby don't worry about this and do not let everybody know your business." My father truly believed that people are not genuinely concerned about you they just want to know your business. I grew up during an era when family business was truly that "family business." In other words, what went on behind closed doors stayed behind those doors.

There was an important person who was a strong force in my life growing up who taught me that it was okay to bring people into your crisis. Every family had their rebels and she was the good kind. My aunt, who was at one point a school teacher, was the person in the family who did not always abide by the rules. Auntie was what we called her but her name was Mary Eliza. She never married and according to my mom Auntie died a virgin. Auntie was a plus size lady very soft spoken, but when opportunity presented itself she could read you your rights. I remember always loving to take daily walks to her home for visits. You could always find her cooking some sort of fancy food or baking something that other households never served. I thought it was fancy because no one in the neighborhood cooked dishes such as blueberry pies, lemon meringue pies, or even strawberry pies. Her tea cakes were like no other and we looked forward to that treat. I was accustomed to pound cakes or sweet potato pies for desert. We only got specialty deserts during the holidays.

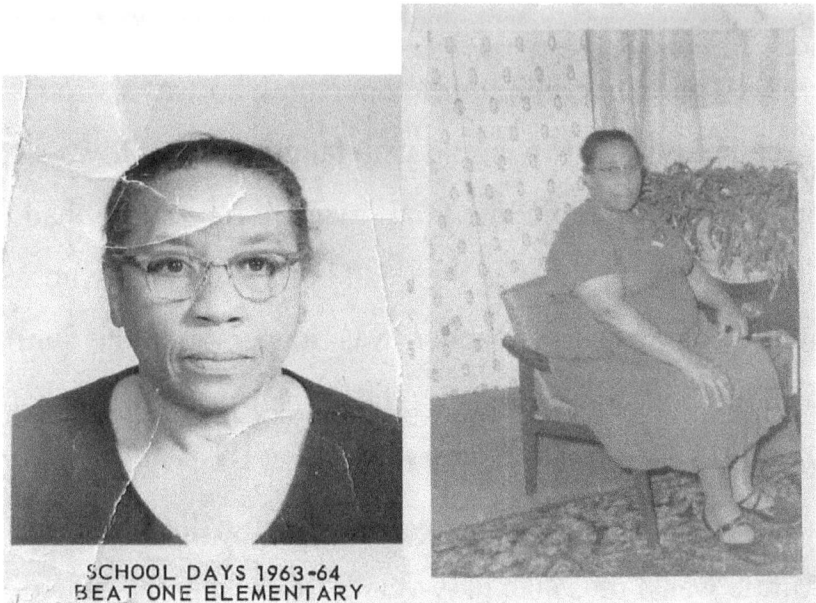

SCHOOL DAYS 1963-64
BEAT ONE ELEMENTARY

(Auntie Mary Eliza)

Auntie always spoke her mind and this would irritate her siblings, especially her brother who lived with her during that time.   Auntie was diagnosed with stomach cancer when I was about nineteen years of age. Everyone was discrete about the health diagnosis, but not her. In fact when you walked into her home, right at the side entrance there was a five drawer dresser that was decorated with a picture of Martin Luther King Jr. on top of the dresser. This is where she kept a newspaper clipping that talked about this disease she was diagnosed with. If you were curious about what her medical condition involved she would have you take that article off the dresser and read it so you could thoroughly understand what she was dealing with. This would always set her brother off. He felt her health issue was no one else's concern. They would exchange a few choice words to each other, but she strongly felt that information was powerful. She was fully aware that her prognosis was grime. Auntie eventually lost her life to the disease. I remember so vividly the courage and strength she possessed. She was neither afraid nor ashamed to show her vulnerable side to people. But nevertheless not many other family members were like her including my father.

My conversation that day with my dad was short and sweet, he told me to take care and put my worries in God's hand. My mother returned to the phone and asked if I wanted her to come to Savannah to be with me. I told her she had her hands full with Daddy and that I would keep her informed of everything that transpired while in the hospital. By the time I ended my conversation with my mother my boss showed up at my home to check on me. I figured the secretary called to inform her of the circumstance. We talked and prayed together. She told me that she would call my pastor to let him know what was going on so that the church could pray for me and my family. By this time the hospital called my home phone to let me know that they had a room available for me. We dropped the children at a friend's home to stay overnight. David and I went to the hospital and settled in for the night.

The next day, I went through numerous tests that included needle biopsy, bone marrow aspirate along with countless blood test. I met my oncologist for the first time and I must admit he did not have any bedside manners. In fact, I was a little skeptical about even having him as a doctor. My red blood count was significantly low which resulted in having to receive a blood transfusion. I must confess I was apprehensive about the transfusion because of the disease known as AIDS. According to the news a number of people contracted the disease through blood transfusions. The nurse however quickly assured me that the blood bank takes the necessary precautions of testing their blood and I need not worry. After the transfusion, I then realized just how much exhaustion had taken over. I was amazed at how much energy I gained from that new blood. The doctor informed me that the following day he scheduled me to have the small lump removed from the side of my neck. That night at the hospital was just like any other night, David and I got very little sleep because of the continuous stream of nurses coming in and out of the room.

Early the next morning I went downstairs to surgery. The surgeon was very nice and kind of cute. He explained details that the procedure would entail and the approximate duration of the surgery. By early afternoon I was back in my room and I also had a few visitors from my job that afternoon. Late that night my pastor and one of the deacons came to visit me at the hospital. I was pretty emotional during their visit. I remember my pastor kneeling down beside my hospital bed asking me why I was so upset. My reply to him was, "I'm afraid of dying." His response to that was, "Regina my Bible says that is the best thing that can happen to you, so again I ask what are you truly upset about." I said to him, "my children are not ready to lose their mother." Pastor's response, "now that makes more sense Mrs. Thompson." Pastor continued to offer me some scriptures to read whenever feeling down and then prayed for me and my family before leaving. The visit turned out to be one that helped me and my husband start to look at things in a different light. We felt that people were showing genuine concern about the well-being of our family. We were learning that even though we did not have immediate family around us in Savannah, we had a host of friends that were surfacing from everywhere to offer their prayers and concerns. It was becoming very obvious that we were not alone after all.

Surprisingly, my middle brother and my sister came up from Mississippi to check on me. There were so many people in the small hospital room on that day that I could not even hear myself think. It was at that moment that everything became so surreal. In that moment, I heard absolutely no noise. David had stepped out a little earlier to pick the children up from school. He brought the children up to my hospital room and as he was walking through the door the phone rang. David had this perplexed look on his face when he entered into the room. I think he was in a state of shock by the number of people that were in the room. I saw my sister who was standing on the opposite side of the bed at the time, Sharon handed him the phone but he just stood there with the phone in his hand with a blank look on his face. I watched him place the phone on the bed and leave the room. A few minutes passed, but he did not return. I then asked my sister who was on the phone and she replied "David's mother", but by this time she obviously hung up because David never answered the phone. I got up, went into the hallway to look for him and found him and the children sitting in the lobby. I asked if he was okay and he said walking into my room with all of those people made him realize just how serious this was. At that very moment, it became surreal and he needed to get out of that space. So he retreated out in the lobby with the children.   This was our opportunity to talk with the children because up to this point they knew very little of what was going on. David and I decided to be open and honest about my reasons for being in the hospital. Devida, my daughter, was full of questions and Jeremiah was a lot like my dad quiet and reserved. My husband did most of the talking, trying to explain as best as he could, what was happening to mommy. Devida asked what cancer was and if I was going to die from this disease. David expressed to her that as a family our concern would be focused only on fighting this disease. He explained that through prayer and leaning heavily on our family support system we'd get through this phase of our life. Jeremiah did not say anything nor did he ask any questions. We assured the children that mommy was going to be fine because we had God on our side. We explained that although we had a tough road ahead of us, we would get through it as a family.

The next day I received a visit in my hospital room from the doctor who was standing in for my Oncologist and the head nurse. He delivered the news about the results of the series of testing I had taken during the week. He explained that I had a disease called (pathology) lymphoma, what it meant and where the disease was located. The areas affected were my esophagus, spleen, groin, and my bone marrow. The doctor insisted that I immediately start an intense round of high dose chemotherapy. Needless to say I had heard about chemo, but really did not have a clear understanding of what it all meant. The nurse seemingly picked up on the fact that I was very overwhelmed with the information just given to me and she suggested to the doctor that I needed to have some time to digest the news given to me. She suggested that I receive the first dose of my chemo later that day or the very next morning. The doctor agreed that I get started the next morning. David and I were able to spend some time discussing what was to be the beginning of a long journey being a cancer patient. We called our families out of town to inform them of the diagnoses and asked them to keep us in their thoughts and prayers. When I called my mom to tell her about the treatments I would encounter in the months to come, she informed me that Daddy had been receiving chemo treatments and she had no idea what was going on. Daddy only told her because he was not doing very well physically with his treatments which caused him to need her to drive to appointments. As usual, Mama offered encouraging words and prayers.

Chapter 3: CHEMOTHERAPY a.k.a CHEMO

The next day seemed to have come faster than it usually does. The nurse came into my room with an intravenous bag that contained a sly blue liquid and explained to me that this was my chemo. She then proceeded to put on gloves that covered her arms up to her elbows. Hesitantly, I asked why she had this armor on. She gave me the daunting details of how harmful this toxic blue fluid (chemo) could be to the top layer of skin. I of course questioned how my veins would be able to handle this medication. She explained that this medication could cause severe nausea. It could even cause me to lose my hair. This information did not help the fear I was already experiencing about getting my first chemo treatment. However, I was very curious about what was to come. David and I watched in silence as the nurse hung this bag onto the IV pole. She then connected the elongated tube to the IV that was taped to my arms. The fluid dripped down into the long tube, then into the needle that rested in my veins. Although I expected some big event to occur immediately, it did not. That was it, my first chemotherapy treatment took about 3.5 hours. An hour later I felt the same. After that, I was given permission to be discharged from the hospital with specific instructions to have two prescriptions filled that would help with nausea.

I was so excited to finally be going home to my children. I felt pretty good so I insisted that we drop off the prescription and David would pick it up later that evening. After a week of being away from my children I was a bit anxious to get there. Upon arrival, I was embraced by my children, sister, brother, and my mother-in-law. I inhaled the aroma of my home and began to feel good about being back into my place of peace. I went upstairs to rest and David returned to work. After a couple of hours of sleep, I awoke feeling extremely ill. I called out to my family downstairs but no one answered. I mustered up enough energy to get out of bed and go to the top of the stairs to call out again; still no answer. I sat down on the top stair because at that point I started to feel faint and my insides felt like they were on fire. I called out once again and this time my brother heard me. My brother and mother-in-law came to my call and my mother-in-law quickly instructed me to get back into the bed. She felt my head and stated that I was very warm so she began placing cool towels across my forehead. I asked my brother to call David and tell him to bring my medication home because I was feeling extremely ill. If I had followed the instructions of the doctor and took the medications as prescribed this could have been avoided, but the excitement of being home was more important than pills. David made it home pretty fast with the medication. Shortly after taking the pills I went to sleep.

The next morning I woke up feeling fairly good, a little sluggish but okay none the less. Surprisingly, I had the pleasure of being graced with a visit from my father-in-law and my brother-in-law who did all the driving. One thing you must know about my father-in-law is that he rarely goes out of town to visit anyone, therefore this was a very pleasant surprise taking into consideration that he did not even make it to our wedding. Some might say that this would be upsetting, but you had to know my father-in-law to understand that he would do just about anything for his family. So I was more than delighted to have my extended family in our home to support us.

That weekend was unforgettable and it showed the importance of family when times get difficult. Having someone to show their support through their presence, love, and concern, seems to carry so much weight. This made it difficult for the journey we were to bark upon. We did not have family in Savannah and that weekend showed us the value of a supportive extended family when facing crisis. Once everyone left we had to prepare for a life that included cancer.

I returned to work that following Monday. This was somewhat awkward because I was confused about how I should feel. I tried to slip into the office without bringing much attention to myself but that proved impossible. I was greeted with a warm welcome from everyone in the office. As that day progressed I had a chance to sit with my supervisor to talk about what was going on with me and what was to come. During our conversation, I made the statement, "Why did this have to happen to me?" The response my boss gave was truly unexpected, she simply replied, "Why not you Regina? I am not trying to be mean or callus, but who are you to feel you're excused from any type of tragedy or hard times.

All of us at some point will face some type of trial in our lives. Your focus now should be to deal with the hand you were dealt. Regina how you handle this will require having a certain kind of attitude and most importantly a strong faith."

This may have seemed harsh to some, but instead of reacting in a negative manner, I decided she was absolutely correct. Things happen to people every day so it was arrogant of me to put myself above life's trials. I reminded myself that the Bible teaches that there will be storms, trials and tribulations, but having unyielding faith is what gets you through those hard times. My boss did commit to being available for me in any way necessary. She also told me not to be worried about my job, but to focus on getting myself healed. I planned my chemotherapy treatments to occur on Fridays so I would have the weekends to recover. This way I would not miss very much work each month.

Treatment included seven chemo treatments, once a month. My first treatment occurred in the hospital. The second one took place at the doctor's office. This was my first visit to my Oncologist's office and the entire staff treated us well. This visit was much better compared to the meet and greet we had in the hospital. He had terrible bedside manners, which gave me a bad impression of him. But once I met with him on his territory (his office) he presented himself as a concerned doctor who had my best interest in mind. He took the time to talk to me and explained what was to come. The advice he shared resonated the most with me. He stated that in order to get through the next few months I needed to have a positive attitude and with that we could beat this thing. This was all too familiar. My boss uttered those same words to me. Dr. Badal made us (myself and David) feel as though everything would be just fine. That was the moment I decided that I had the power over how I would respond to my diagnoses. Dr. Badal talked to me about what to expect in during my monthly treatments. I was told that I would lose my hair due to the type of medication prescribed. There would be nausea and possible vomiting for which I would receive medications to help alleviate the symptoms. He also mentioned that there would be moments of low blood counts preceding treatments and that I needed to take precautions to protect myself from infections. Prednisone would be prescribed to help with the healing process after my chemotherapy. After my visit with the doctor, I was escorted by a nurse to the chemotherapy room.

We walked into a space that had the appearance of a community room with several nice recliners that were aligned along the walls of the room. The nurse's station was located in the center of the room overlooking the patients receiving chemo. I was seated in one of the recliners and my nurse introduced himself to me. He was a red head who obviously worked out and he had beautiful smile, not to mention a beautiful attitude that followed. He made my husband and I feel very comfortable. Before the treatment starts you are given a shot of Benadryl. This usually put me to sleep during the three and a half hour long treatment. My husband patiently sat through the treatments for the entire session. The day usually ended with taking medication for nausea. Saturday was spent in bed feeling nauseated and weak. Sunday I was in and out of bed tolerating ginger ale, crackers, and soft foods. Monday I was able to report to work.

As a working wife and mother, chemotherapy

became a forced part of my life. Keeping the children's schedule in mind and trying to miss little work were factors that had to be taken into consideration when setting up the treatments. This was a prime example that life does not pause when obstacles arise. My mother usually kept my children during the summer months because this was their time to spend with the children. This summer she wanted things to remain the same. She felt that the children would be able to help her out with caring for my dad while he was receiving treatments. We took the children to Mississippi and I saw my dad for the first time since finding out he had lymphoma. Dad did not speak much about his diagnoses which was not unusual for him. He encouraged me to take care of myself and not involve many people in my business as always.

Keeping our lives private is something my dad strongly believed in. Daddy was a proud man who felt he was the only one capable of taking care of his family and himself. Sharing his emotions was not a quality he possessed anger and frustration were what we witnessed from him throughout our lives. As I can recall, I only saw my dad cry once when my little sister was young and she fell off of a wagon pulled by a horse. She cracked her skull from one ear to the other and the prognosis was grime. Although she survived, that was the only time I can remember seeing my Dad cry. Cancer appeared to have a strong presence on Daddy's side of the family. So many family members were diagnosed with some form of cancer and died as a result. The only family member I could remember having a positive and fighting attitude was my aunt. I remember a number of relatives pretty much receiving their cancer diagnosis and retreating into their homes accepting death as their faith. I watched my Dad follow that same pattern. Daddy once told me that he could not understand why most of his family refused to fight for their lives. He mastered fighting to take care of his family by any means necessary. After being diagnosed with cancer he did not feel this was something he could control or fight. That summer, I exposed to my Dad how telling people about my journey opened doors to resources and blessings. It also allowed me to hear the testimonies of others'. We left the children with mom and dad that year and he seemed to find his zest for life again. Especially with my son who was his first grandchild.

According to my mom Jeremiah took charge of caring for my dad, after we left.

Chapter 4: DADDY

We returned to our regularly scheduled program in Savannah and cancer was still there waiting on me. Treatments continued as usual and Dr. Badal voiced his surprise about me not losing my hair. At the end of that summer we went to Mississippi to get the children and it was at that time I could see that cancer was starting to take a physical toll on Daddy. He became even more of a recluse. Mom said that he did not want people coming over to see how he looked. Dad was a strikingly handsome man and not just because he was my dad. He had a caramel skin, black silky hair (good hair as the African community refers to it) with Native American features. When cancer attacked his looks he did not want the public, which included family and friends to see him.

Daddy called a family meeting with my brothers. I included myself because dad would have never involved me. They discussed how the property would be distributed and he wanted to ensure the land stayed in the family instead of daughter-in-laws or son-in-laws getting the property and selling it off to strangers. Daddy felt that he struggled too hard to allow the land to slip into the hands of anybody who would not appreciate the property. He had seen what happens when a family member dies and the children sell the land to strangers because they had no desire to return back to Mississippi. This was the first sign that showed us things were about to change. Then he came to the subject of changing doctors or at least getting a second opinion. We all agreed that he needed to do what his heart was leading him to. The decision was made. He decided to go to the Jackson Mississippi Memorial Hospital for a second opinion. This was a surprise to all, but a well needed discussion. We all returned to our homes for the weekend and it was understood that Mom would take Daddy to Jackson Mississippi Memorial Hospital.

(From left to right, Regina, sis Sharon, dad Melvin)

After we departed, my middle brother shared that Daddy carried on as if we never discussed or agreed that he would seek out other options for medical attention. He explained that he, my half-brother and older cousin went to visit Daddy almost every day trying to persuade him to get help elsewhere, but he continued to resist. Daddy had apparently stopped eating and drinking liquids. Keith stated that he reached his breaking point and decided that he did not want to allow Daddy to sit around and die. He made up his mind to take Daddy for help with or without his approval. Although this was a two hour drive from the house, Keith felt this was necessary. Daddy did not have the physical strength to fight, but he used his words to express his disapproval. Daddy cursed and yelled out that Keith was killing him and then fell into complete silence. He zoned out, suddenly absent from any emotion just a flat affect. This scared my brother so he changed his course of action and took Daddy to the local hospital. The tests revealed that Daddy's sugar levels had dropped dangerously low and that explained his lack of emotion. Once they were able to get Daddy's sugar back up Keith drove him to Jackson to allow a different medical team to look at Daddy.

Mom called to let us know that the doctors in Jackson admitted Daddy to the hospital and did a series of tests. By the end of the week the tests revealed that Daddy's body was seriously damaged from the previous chemotherapy treatments and the doctor was concerned about doing any immediate treatments because of his physical and mental state. Instead the doctor decided to give his body some time to heal before starting a new treatment. Dr. Mike was puzzled by the fact that Daddy's physical state was severely damaged. Dr. Mike had many discussions with my father, but Daddy would not say very much to him. One morning Dr. Mike visited my dad and he was shocked at how daddy greeted him with such a warm and inviting welcome. He actually told my dad and mom that he thought he was a mute because daddy never spoke to him. Daddy started to share many intimate conversations with the doctor. Daddy shared all about his children and grandchildren. He talked to him about the work he was doing for the small community church he was a Steward for and the things he was doing to help the church grow. He shared with Dr. Mike that he was not a strong man he was a weak man. His worst fear was his wife having to take care of him and that was something he could not handle. He took pride in being the head of his family supporting his wife and children not the other way around. Dr. Mike explained to Daddy that the cancer would not kill him; his heart would give out first. He pleaded with Daddy to release some of the things he was harboring and allow other people to help him for a change. Daddy told Dr. Mike that he asked God to take him and spare his daughter who is fighting cancer also. He wanted his girl to raise her children because they needed their mother. Dr. Mike soon began a much milder treatment that required Daddy to stay at the hospital after the treatments, but complications soon followed. Multiple transfusions had to be administered and the decision was made to basically make him as comfortable as possible. This went on for several weeks. I made a trip down to see Daddy and was in total shock at how much weight he had lost.

It became apparent that Mama was not revealing the severity of Daddy's illness. He appeared as a skeleton, during my first visit to the hospital. She expressed that he had become bitter towards her. When I entered his hospital room I gasped at the sight of his frail body. I did my best not to show my expression and instead gave a warm greeting. Not soon after arriving, I witnessed what my mother meant by his attitude being blatant and insensitive. He started to say some pretty mean things to my mom about something ridiculous. I asked him why he was being so mean towards her and his anger quickly turned towards me. He even threatened to have security remove me from the hospital. I walked outside his room and started wailing. My sister-in-law did her best to comfort me, but I was feeling too much pain at that time. The shock of his physical appearance and the resentment and anger that had taken over his mind was just too much to bare. I composed myself and went back into the room and started to share with him some of the things that I took comfort in when I was not at my best mentally nor physically. I shared a Bible verse with him and started to read out loud, when out of nowhere he began to moan so loud letting me know in other words he was not interested. This was not like my dad. He was in a state that I could not understand or could relate to.

This trip was very difficult for me mentally and physically. I had to get back home to take my chemo treatment and the trip took so much energy out of me that my doctor was concerned about my state of mind. Dr. Badal encouraged me to be careful of stress because this could impact my healing in a negative way. Eventually, I called my Mom and had the most difficult conversation I have ever had with her. I told her how much I loved her and how much I wanted to be there to help her, but I was not strong enough to keep coming home for that nine hour drive, being subjected to Daddy's explosive angry outbursts, and coming back home to do my chemotherapy. I told her that I had to be there for her in prayer. As always she was understanding and only asked that I take care of myself. Each phone call I made home to check on dad I focused on being as positive as I could when talking to him. He would say very little when he would get on the phone. Each time I spoke with him his voice seemed to get weaker and weaker. I became very concerned for my mother. She was not leaving Daddy's hospital room very much. I convinced her to ask if there were groups within the hospital that she could attend to help with her mentally.

The nurses told her about a group that met in the hospital. The group consisted of Care Givers of loved ones dealing with a major illness. My mother's tone changed once she started attending the meetings. Daddy was not too happy with her leaving him for that hour each day, but it gave her the motivation to venture outside of the hospital, even if it was just walking in the court yard or across the street for a meal. She tried many times to get him to go, but he was not interested.

One day she decided to take a trip home because she had not been home for almost a month. There were things that needed to be taken care of and she also wanted to check on the house and pay some of the bills. To her surprise he was okay with her going home. He even told her to spend the night home and Cousin Willie would stay with him. She got home and went to her hair stylist to get her hair done and shortly after being there she received a call from a family member saying that Daddy had turned for the worst. She packed up and went back to the hospital, she did not even think to call and find out what was going on. Upon her return he was sitting up in the hospital bed talking to Cousin Willie. They asked why she returned so soon and she told them about the phone call she received. She decided to not go back through the trouble of taking the two hour drive home again and stayed at the hospital. Daddy's health continued to decline, but his attitude improved greatly. Before I knew it, I received the call no one ever wants to get, mom called stating that Dr. Mike felt we should all come home.

I tried not to think the obvious, since I had been praying so hard for a miracle to happen. Daddy had made so many improvements over the past few years, before cancer came. Daddy was a hard man, always serious about everything he did. I remember calling home one time and he answered the phone, well this was totally out of character for him because he rarely ever picked up the phone even if he was sitting next to it when it rang. It was a treat talking to daddy over the phone for more than five minutes. This particular call was because I was in need of advice in regards to my marriage. Normally, this was always a conversation with my mom, this time it was with my dad. The phone call turned into an hour long conversation which was unheard of but I loved every minute. He even revealed to me one phone conversation that he was curious why we would get Mama nice Christmas gifts and he would get the same old things, ties or shirts. He said that he liked jewelry too. Well needless to say I bought him his first rope chain. He got his first colored television after this and many more nice gifts as he would call them. When that phone call came it carried great heaviness.

Most of us got in on that Thursday and the rest came on Friday. My older brother and I spent that

Thursday with him and we went home with the intentions of getting the house together because mama had been away from the house for about a month now. We wanted to clean, dust and knock down the cob webs to prepare the house for daddy to possibly come home for a visit. Friday came and the plans were to spend most of the day working on the house and go to the hospital Saturday to visit with Daddy. For some reason, that day I felt a strong urge to pay Daddy a visit. I asked my brothers if they would be interested in also going at the end of the day. I could not get any of my brothers to agree to drive the two hours to the hospital. Everyone wanted to wait. I kept on insisting and finally Calvin, my oldest brother, agreed to take me.

We made it to the hospital late in the afternoon and my mother reported that Daddy had been talking about how proud he was of us all day. She said he especially wanted to talk to me. I walked over to my father lying in bed who once stood 6'1', beautiful black silky hair, and 200lbs, who was now bald, frail, and hardly 120lbs. I took his hand and asked what he needed to tell me. He had this gentle smile with water in his eyes, but was not able to say anything. Mama said he was so full of life earlier, but he never said a word to me or my brother. I asked if he was ready to come home and he just softly said he could not come home. I asked if he wanted something to eat, and began to I feed him a bowl of soup. Calvin stood alongside the bed for a few hours just holding his hands. Night fall quickly came and Calvin announced it was time to get back up that dark road. We said our "I love you's and "goodbye's." Our mother walked us out into the hall way. Once we got outside the door, I heard my father yell out for mama saying that he was defecating on himself and he needed help. My mother disappeared back into the hospital room and we got back on the road heading home.

The conversation seemed to go in an unintentional direction. We started chatting about the rural community that Mom lives in and the fact that there were no street lights on the country road. My brother and I decided that we needed to get street lights put up around Mama's house when she comes home. We also stated that it would be smart to put on the windows around the house. Something in me noticed we spoke of Daddy as if he would never return home. I said to my brother it was like we put

Daddy in the grave and we just left Mama and Daddy at the hospital. I wanted to remember that although he was very weak he was still alive. It was late when we returned so we went to bed. Before day break the phone rang and I sat up in the bed knowing that something was wrong on the other end of the phone. I refused to pick the phone up so Craig answered the phone and I could hear him say, "hello, uh huh, I see and okay." When he hung up he announced that our cousin called to say that Daddy was having trouble breathing and we needed to get to the hospital. Craig, Calvin, Keith, Mark, Metric, and I boarded the van and took that long drive to Jackson Mississippi Memorial Hospital. My sister Sharon who lived in Oxford was informed of the circumstances and arranged to come join us. The two hour drive was quiet, no one spoke a word. I offered everyone some mints or gum and each of them quietly held their hands out to accept the breath fresheners, but still no one uttered one single word. We finally arrived at the hospital; we parked my brothers van and took that long walk up to his hospital room.

We walked into the room and Daddy was lying in

the bed, but this time he had a white towel tied around the base of his jaw line around his entire head. I don't remember who said or if someone said at that time he was deceased. Calvin and I walked up to his bed side and took his hand which had a clammy feel to it. We both said his name very softly, but he did not respond, we said it again and I believe it was at that time someone said he is gone. I turned to them and asked, "what do you mean", by this time Calvin faced the hospital wall crying out as though he was in pain and the rest of my siblings in the room followed pursuit in this intense display of emotions. This went on for several minutes and once things started to settle down some Mama started to talk about his last moments before taking his last breathe and by this time Sharon and her family made it to the hospital. She walked over to Daddy's bedside as we did earlier and she took his hand and again called out to him anxiously waiting for him to respond. I whispered, "Sharon he is gone." She shook him a few more times and finally she accepted that his life had transitioned.

Mama again started to tell us about his last moments with her. She said that after Calvin and I left the hospital yesterday evening daddy's attention went to being concerned with how she was doing. According to her he asked several times if she was going to be okay. She said she realized that he was ready to let go so she consoled him by telling him she was going to be okay. He then proceeded to tell her to lie down close her eyes and go to sleep. She said they went back and forth about not being sleepy and she again came to the conclusion he was trying to leave her so she did what he asked. She said she cracked opened her eyes after a short while and that is when she witnessed him taking his last breathes of life. Mama stated that the nurses came in and started the revival process and she said not to. She said to us that our father was tired and was ready to "Go Home to Glory" and she did not want to selfishly keep him here to continue to suffer. She gave him her permission to move on. As hard as it was to hear this, I understood because Daddy was no longer the man we grew up with. Cancer stripped him of his physical appearance and it almost took his spirit, but he was able to find that spirit before closing his eyes and we could not have asked for a better ending.

Daddy looked so peaceful lying in that hospital bed.

There was no stress in his face just a peaceful sleep like state. We all sort of lingered around going in and out of the room calling our loved ones to give the bad news. A group of men came and I could not watch them prepare to escort his body out of the hospital. So I disappeared into the waiting room, my brothers and my mom supervised this tribulation. At some point the coroner allowed my family to say good bye and they processed my dad's body to be taken out of the hospital.

We then left the hospital loaded back into my brothers van and headed back to my mother's house. Again this two hour trip was silent and long. When we arrived back in my mom's community, pulling up to the house we could see that there was a sea of cars and people. We were greeted with so much love. The aroma of food filled the house. My mother was exhausted and the first thing she did was announce that she was going to take a bath. I believe some of her sisters agreed to assist her with washing the weeks and weeks of living at the hospital off of her tired body. My siblings dispersed out and about in the crowd of people not to seem anti-social even though we were all mentally and physically drained.

I remember being out in the yard and conversing with my Dad's youngest sister and the dreaded realization came over me that Daddy would not be visiting me ever again at my Savannah home. I blurted out "Oh my God who's gonna visit me at Christmas time this year." My aunt had this blank look on her face. She tried to comfort me, but it did not work well. My dad's family was never great at sharing emotions or showing much love towards me and my siblings. My dad's sister did not care very much for us. In fact, some even said we were not all Daddy's' children because some of us were light skinned like my parents and a couple of my brothers were more of a medium/dark brown complexion. One of my cousins made an announcement that later got back to my mom that she did not have to be recognized or treated like family since Uncle Melvin died. My mother was never moved by this because she had endured so much from them that she welcomed not being bothered by their drama. I eventually moved away from my aunt and strolled back into the house where my mother, her mom and guests were gathered in me and my sisters' old bedroom. They joked around as if to purposely ignore the elephant in the room

which was the death of Daddy. At some point, the house
was filled with so many people that the noise of all the
different conversations became overwhelming. I
remember thinking that if Daddy were here it would not
be so loud. Just as that was going through my mind the
lights flickered throughout the house and a dead silence
came over the house. Someone shouted out that Melvin
was telling us we are being too loud and believe it or not
people actually began to use their inside voices. Once
things calmed down Cousin Janie pulled us all together to
let us know that the funeral home would be coming over
in the next day or two to meet with us on making the
arrangements for Daddy's home going. This was our first
time making arrangements for a funeral, but family
members were fairly good at preparing us for what was to
come. Mom announced that she was leaving all the
decisions to us because her job as his wife was complete.
Personally, I feel as though she was simply exhausted and
could not deal with the funeral arrangements. She had
been nursing Daddy for the past year therefore she handed
the torch off to us. After our guests left we reposed for the
evening. It was hard to rest so I got up during the early

hours to watch television only to find my mom, sister and older brother sitting in the living room talking. We shared with one another the shock of being in the process of planning out father's funeral. Mom talked about the past few months nursing daddy. She shared her struggles with having to watch his decline, but she also shared her happiness with his faith returning before closing his eyes. We shared stories until the sunlight greeted us.

The funeral home staff came out that morning to meet with us and they gave the instructions of what role we would play in preparation for Daddy's transition. The funeral home director shared that he has experienced years of preparing individuals for their final transition. He has seen bodies in all types of conditions but it was apparent by the expression on Daddy's face that he wore his halo on his head. We completed the task of making the arrangements with the funeral home director. A family member assisted us with getting all the information together for the obituary. The funeral home required a final viewing of the body from the family members which usually takes place the day before the actual service. This also allowed the community to come in and pay their last respects for those who might not attend the funeral.

We also met with our father's best friend and decisions were made to put bars on mom's windows and street lights outside the house now that she would be living alone. During the week leading up to the funeral, various members in the community agreed to look out for Mama to ensure she remained safe. A couple of our aunts (dad's sisters) who rarely engaged in conversation with us, volunteered to purchase me and Sharon's (my sister) dresses for the funeral. This was an odd experience because hanging out with Daddy's family was a rare occasion. Conversing with them was even more so awkward at best, but good even though it took an occasion such as this to unite us. It was generous of them to do it, even if it was for our dad's funeral. My mom was the only one who ever asked or inquired about my cancer issue while we were planning Daddy's funeral. She also inquired about my next chemotherapy appointment, since I was behind a couple of weeks for my last chemotherapy. Just so happened my oncologist called to let me know that I was now two weeks behind on my scheduled chemotherapy treatment. He offered his condolences, but urged me that it was important not to get too much more behind.

The day to lay our dad to rest came very quickly. Not much talking took place about Daddy on this day; it was like that topic was off limits. Our focus was on planning to make the day successful for our guests. I know that the religion states that we mourn a birth and celebrate a death, but it still feels wrong to call it a celebration. The funeral cars arrived to pick us up and that is when it became surreal. The process seemed prolonged or maybe I just wished this situation was not happening. This was the final time we would see our father which was tough to accept. I kept telling myself that it was important that we represented to the community that we honored his life. As we arrived to the church, I noticed when we exited the funeral home cars all eyes turned to the family. Perhaps they were looking for our reaction or response once we took that last walk or viewing of daddy's body before they closed his casket. Daddy said several times while living that he wanted a closed casket funeral because he felt that people attended these types of events just to see how that person looks after being ill. But the decision was made to have an open casket service anyhow. A slew of overwhelming emotions came rushing to me while approaching his body down at the front of the church. I was able to keep it together because I could hear daddy saying don't cry for me, I am in a better place so be happy for me. While I stood over my dad's casket, I was struck with the realization that the cancer Daddy died from was the exact invader which still resided in my body. It became crystal clear that this disease was a force to be reckoned with. Standing over his lifeless body I said,

> *"Daddy, I prayed so hard to God asking him to spare your life and to take mine. It was so beautiful watching you finally embrace the things around you after years watching you drilling through life so hard and so diligently to the point of missing what beauty life had to offer. I will miss your visits to me in Savannah. I will miss waiting on you hand and foot so that you enjoyed just resting while visiting. I will miss preparing you different dishes trying to impress you or just share things I knew you had not tried before. I want you to know Daddy that I will beat this cancer thing for the both of us, I love you so much and you will be missed tremendously. We will take care of mom for you so don't worry about her. I hate that you will miss your*

grandchildren growing up, but I know you
will be watching over us. I guess you will be
our family's Guardian Angel. Rest now
Daddy and when God is ready I will see you
again. Love you Daddy."

Melvin Thompson
October 5, 1940/September 30, 1995
"The just man walketh in his integrity:
His children are blessed after him."
Proverbs 20:7

Once we were seated and I got my breath back and pulled my sentiments together I looked around and saw that the church was jam-packed. People were standing up because there was not any seating left; I remember hearing someone say that the parking lot was filled with even more people. My attention was quickly stolen by a family member who while viewing Daddy's body truly made a scene. He yelled out, "why God took Melvin from us and why did God not take me." This went on for a few minutes until someone sympathetically grabbed him by his arm and led him down the aisle to his seat. I did not even recognize this person so I leaned over to ask Mom who he was. She shared that it was one of Daddy's nephews who we had not seen in years. I then noticed that there were quite a few Caucasian people in the congregation whom I had never seen before. Mommy later shared that the factory where Daddy was employed actually closed during the time of the funeral and it was mandatory for the employees/staff scheduled that day to attend the funeral to pay their respect. The pastor gave a wonderful eulogy for our father. The funeral was over and the next daunting task was watching the actual closing of his casket. This is a pain that hit deep in my core and I became well aware this was the very last time I would see Daddy. I fixed in my mind somehow that the body in the casket is not the man that shared in our lives for the number of years we had him. That body was just the vessel that was used while he was with us on earth.

The next difficult event involved going to the grave site to awkwardly watch them lower Daddy's body into the ground. I did not want to go, but I had to for my mother. Surprisingly yet again, I kept it together with just soft whispers of tears. After the funeral was over the family usually spends time with guests who graced the bereaving family with their appearance at the loved one's funeral. Unfortunately, I did not have the courage for this so I tried to work my way off the church grounds, and was stopped by a few high school friends. I took a few minutes to offer my gratitude for their support. It was a good feeling to know they thought enough of our family to pay their respect. We made it home and all the food and people at the house were overwhelming. Friends and family invested a lot of time and energy to help feed the wonderful individuals who showed their love to us. The day ended magnificently and we were all exhausted.

This was probably the first night we had absolutely no problem falling asleep, but it was short lived. Around 3 a.m. the neighborhood alcoholic who also happened to be a relative, arrived unannounced at moms' house beating on our door. He was yelling extremely loud demanding that mom give him some food. My oldest brother who is military with a body builder physique jolted open the front door and bellowed, "What the hell do you want." Pooh was his name, he was startled by my brother he quickly apologized then ran off. My brother exclaimed to him never to return to our mothers' home again or he would shoot him. I could recall Daddy saying those same words to him years ago when he walked into our home and took money off of the bedroom dresser. Pooh refused to return it, until I informed my father of his roguish action. Daddy only asked him once if he took the money and of course his reply was "no". Daddy then followed it up by forcing Pooh to put the money back and never set foot on the property again or he would be shot. He handed Daddy the money, apologized and vacated the property. It was just ironic that he picked the most inopportune time to visit the property again. We spent a few more days with Mom to assist with emptying Daddy's closet and securing the house. The time came for us to leave; it was also time for me to continue my fight against cancer.

Chapter 5: FALSE CLEAR...2ND TIME'S A CHARM

Shortly after returning home and getting back into the swing of things, I received my last chemotherapy treatment. A few weeks later various blood tests and X-rays were administered and it appeared that I was in the clear. My oncologist scheduled my follow-up appointment in about six months to check on the status and instructed me if I had any symptoms to appear before the follow-up to come in. We made the effort to settle back into our normal routine, but my stress level changed somewhat and it was hard to express my emotions with my husband. It was a challenge to get used to the cancer free life. It was hard for me to grieve for my dad, since I have a tendency to keep issues inside and that seems to be my life pattern. In order to cope, my focus shifted from my life issues to helping someone in need. Ignoring issues at hand and finding other priorities is how I masked the more important topics.

A friend of mine was experiencing changes with her husband that became too volatile for her and their children to at home, therefore, I extended my home until she could devise a plan. I felt compelled to help because similar to David and myself, she was without family in Savannah for assistance. We went from a four person home to a seven person home. This situation was not an inconvenience because my mom always said she would do for others the way she wanted others to do for her children if they ever needed help. This was reciprocal of the environment I was nurtured in. It was natural for me to reach out to a person in need. During this time, I noticed some of the symptoms returning, but I ignored it. I figured maybe my body was trying to adjust after going through the toxic regimen of chemotherapy. Time came for me to have my six month follow up.   During my visit with Dr. Badal, he asked how I was overall and about family as always. He was a doctor who never made you feel things were doom and gloomy, it was always positive which is why I grew to have such great respect for him. I never mentioned that some of the same symptoms had returned. He ordered the many blood tests and x-rays. Dr.

Badal told me and David that he would let us know if there were any problems with my test results, and if I did not hear from him in about a week things were good.

At the end of the week as we returned home from the workday, the phone rang. Things were hectic inside of the house since Mandy's toddler was very fussy and it was hard getting him to quiet down. As the phone rang, the caller ID showed that Dr. Badal's office was calling, but I did not have it in me to pick it up so David answered. All I could hear was a lot of yes sirs, I understand and we will. When he hung up the phone I went straight into the kitchen to start dinner. I overheard David ask Mandy to take her son to another room, but still the crying was still pretty loud so David asked me to come out into the back yard. He told me that Dr. Badal said the cancer was back more aggressively this time. He scheduled an appointment for the upcoming Monday to discuss what approach he had in mind. Of course I listened, when he was finished talking I simple replied that I had to get dinner started. I did not put too much attention that weekend to the phone call other than calling my mother to inform her of what was going on. She was always the first person I would call on whenever something major occurred and I did not have a clue how to approach it. She recommended finding out what the doctors' advice was.

Monday finally came and David and I sat before Dr. Badal and we listened to his findings. He explained that the cancer was returning so quickly causing it to be a more bellicose category which meant the new treatment would be more aggressive. He informed us of our two options including completing another round of intense chemotherapy or being my own donor in what is called a stem cell transplant. He explained that another name for the process was autologous stem cell transplant and that it uses stem cells from my body. He presented me with the option of having the treatment locally (Savannah) or I could go to the medical center in Atlanta. Dr. Badal explained that the process involved separating the mature cells from the stem cells (baby or immature cells) from my body. He did however make it known that there was a very small chance of missing cells and the disease could possibly be re-introduced back into my body through the same process. With this being an experimental transplant there was not examples or cases to compare this to give me a percentage of survival rates. He advised me that several trips to the hospital receiving high dose chemotherapy to destroy as many cancer cells as possible would be necessary. Then a harvest would be performed for the transplant to take place. He also informed me that this time I would definitely lose my hair. Dr. Badal said that this would be a difficult road to travel, but he needed me to be strong and to have a positive mind throughout the process. He assured me and David that he would be present every step of the way.

Without question, immediately we chose to conduct the transplant at home since we felt this was the only thing that made sense because it would allow our children's lives and everyday schedule to remain fairly the same. We began preparation for my transplant in Savannah. I shared the decision with my mom and she understood and respected my choice. Before the first round of chemotherapy, I needed to have a Port-a-catheter implanted into a large vein of my chest which was situated just above my heart. The catheter helped to alleviate the pain when needles were inserted into my arms or hands during infusions or when blood was drawn. Per my doctor the catheter provided a route in, by which all my medications, blood products, and nutritional supplements would be administered painlessly and a route out, by which blood would be withdrawn for the samples that would be needed throughout my hospital stay. Once I healed from this procedure we scheduled the first of many high dose chemotherapy treatments for my upcoming transplant. My family from Mississippi called to tell me they would be coming to visit me around the time of my first treatment.

This time around the intense chemotherapy took the breath out of me. The aftermath of chemotherapy treatment the first time took a few hours to hit me, this time it hit me immediately. Raising my head off the bed was a challenge in itself. I remember when my mother called the hospital to let us know when they would be arriving. The familiar tone in my husband's voice indicated that something was wrong. After he hung up, I asked what was wrong and of course he said, "Nothing." I looked at him and asked if my father's brother just died. David looked at me with this puzzled look. He shook his head as if to say "yes he did." He asked, "How did I know?" My response was "an odd feeling came over me just in hearing the tone in his voice as he engaged in conversation over the phone". This was another one of my Dad's family members who was diagnosed with cancer. I knew my uncle was ill with cancer, but did not keep up with the status of his condition because I had so much going on in my personal life during that time. My mother made it to Savannah before I was discharged from the hospital. When she entered my room, the look on her face was the same fear I saw when she was nursing my dad. They were trying to extend my recovery in the hospital until I felt strong enough to go home. Eventually, I made up my mind that I needed to be home in order for that to happen especially after my family arrived. I had the nurse ask Dr. Badal to discharge me. I pleaded with him that being in my own home around my support system was what I needed to get better. My mother kept asking me to wait until I was stronger before trying to rush home. I simply expressed to her that my home is my sanctuary and I knew being there surrounded by the love was the only place that would make me feel better. Keep in mind I could barely hold my head off the pillow at that time, but after much begging he agreed to release me. He urged me to return if things became too difficult. When the hospital transport came to get me, I needed help getting into the wheel chair. The movement from rolling me down the hallways of the hospital and the elevator ride gave me a horrible feeling, but I did not care, home is what my body was yearning for.

Once at home David helped me up the stairs and after my head hit the pillow, I immediately fell into a deep slumber. Sunday morning when I awoke in my own home and bed, I worked my way downstairs where my family was gathered and I realized how good it felt. I was still weak, but just being in the company of my family in my own home surrounded by love made all the difference. David tried to feed me, but my appetite only allowed me to eat very little. Mama announced that they were going back home but before her departure she insisted that I eat a little more. Unfortunately, I was unable to eat. It was hard for me to watch them leave and I could see on her face that it was more difficult for her. Once she returned to Starkville, she called to let us know they made it home and she asked if I ate any more that day. She shared with me that leaving was the hardest thing for her, especially knowing that I was not eating much. This brought back the memory of when Daddy stopped eating in the hospital and it was very difficult for her to see me doing the same. She did say my voice sounded much stronger and that made her feel good. She encouraged me to force myself to eat no matter how hard it was. "Nourishing my body with food would help deal with the intense treatments a whole lot better", she said.

I felt better so I tried to resume the normal schedule of going back to work, but quickly realized that this time around things would have to be tremendously different. I was not doing well at my job because my energy level was very poor. I was struggling to keep up with things around the house. The stress obviously was apparent to my husband. One night after work, David asked what was going on with me. He wanted to know why our conversation had ceased. We sat on the bed that evening and I began to cry. For the first time, I cried on my husband's shoulder and the flood gates opened for the both of us. I told him I was afraid, I did not know what to do, or what to think, or how to act. I felt completely lost.

He shared those same sentiments. He did ask that I lean more on him and stop trying to take on the world by myself. He assured me that he would be on this journey with me all the way. It was at that moment in which we both surrendered to God and asked direction in our lives. That night before bed I said a prayer,

"God I am so grateful for you, but I am calling out to you, I need you more than ever. This is hard Father and I am lost. I am getting out of my own way to let you take over the driver's seat throughout this journey you feel I need to be a part of. I pray for strength, guidance, protection and healing. Please Father help my family through this, give them what they need to handle the road ahead. I am slowing down, taking a pause God so that I can focus on what it is you need me to do, what you need me to hear and/or what you need me to see. Whatever your will is for me I accept. I accept that this battle is not mine God it belongs to you and I gladly surrender it all to you. I plead the blood of Jesus over my entire family, In Jesus name I pray Amen. "

Chapter 6: NEW SPIRITUAL JOURNEY-OVERDRIVE

This was the start of life changing events; this was the start of my Spiritual Journey. The next couple of week's life shifted into overdrive. A chain of events occurred that all worked for the benefit of my entire family. It appeared that this was my season to see Gods favor. David and I made a collective decision to take a leap of faith. We did what we rarely ever did and that was rely on each other for help and share what we were going through with those who cared and wanted to help. This is when I no longer saw my diagnosis (disease) as a death sentence, but instead as a new beginning. I knew that things would be hard, but I also knew that I had God on my side and the love from a support group so tightly linked that it was unbreakable.

One thing that was very apparent, I learned that I did not develop the tools necessary to manage my stress. David and I made the decision that I would take a leave of absence from my job. When I started that job something led me in the direction to take out short and long term disability. This of course was something I had never done on past jobs, but that gut instinct pushed me in the direction of signing up for the insurance. This one decision worked in my favor. It allowed me to put work on hold and focus solely on the part of my life I needed most; my health. My spirit was telling me that the time to put the energy in healing my mind. I focused on becoming confident that God would deliver by healing my body. I knew I had to take this journey for these events to occur and I would come out a stronger person.

After taking a leave of absence from my job life became a little lighter on me. I began to notice the affects the treatment was having on my physical appearance. I started to notice a change in my hair texture a week or so after my treatment. By the end of this week my hair literally felt like wire. It was a Friday night, I stood in the shower and positioned myself under the shower head to wash my hair and that's when it happened. My hair started to peel off my head. It was as if I was taking off a cap in slow motion, but the cap was my hair and hysteria hit. David ran upstairs and came into the bath room. He looked at me and said with this simple look on his face, "Why are you crying, Dr. Badal told you your hair was going to come out." I said to him, "just because someone tells you something is going to happen does not mean you will know how that feels until it actually does happen." My five year old came into the bathroom while David was shaving the rest of my hair off. She looked up at me with crocodile tears flowing from my eyes and said with her sweet voice, "Mommy don't cry, you are still beautiful. It is not the hair that makes a person beautiful; it's what's inside that person that makes them beautiful. Look at it this way, when you get up in the morning you don't have to worry about fixing your hair, you just get up and go." That moment was my first lesson in vanity which came from a little five year old. I remember the clarity I experienced at that moment which was that life is about how you choose to feel when a situation is thrust upon you. You have the key to control how you react to any given situation. Even if it takes your breath away for a few moments you can gather yourself or regroup to get back on your feet.

After losing all of my hair I decided to shop for

wigs, but because of the constant perspiration caused by the cancer symptoms it was hard to keep one on. I found a couple of cool hats that made me look fly. During my last visit to my job to gather things out of my desk, the staff was curious to see how I looked without my hat. Since I actually felt really comfortable taking off the fly hat for them, I did so. To their amazement every one expressed that I looked great bald. Being that my daughter had already shared that I was still beautiful, this, of course, did not come as a surprise to me.

Being at home now gave me time to take care of some things and it allowed me to see things that were occurring that I had not given any attention. For example, my good friend at the time Ms. Deidra was not visiting as normal. I started noticing that she was rarely coming around or returning my calls. I had another friend who came to visit me at my home one day and standing at the door talking to her she asked if I would put my hat on because being bald made it to real for her that I had cancer. I couldn't get mad at her because one of the things I realized about people, they say some of the dumbest things when they are in an uncomfortable position. Of course I did not put on my hat, I just explained to her that when a person steps into my home you must accept what you get or not come into my house. She apologized and she came in and we hung out for a moment. David and I noticed that when people would call and check on me they would all seem to have a story to tell about some relative of theirs who had cancer. The stories all seemed to end with that person dying as a result. After a certain point David would tell people who called to only bring positive energy or uplifting words of encouragement to me. He wanted them to understand that we needed only good energy during this journey we were on. I would correct people when they called and said, "I heard you were sick." I would correct them or have my family correct whoever was inquiring about me that I was not sick, but that cancer was only there temporarily. I expressed that the treatments made me feel sick. I did not want to be labeled as a sick person, but instead as someone who was determined to recuperate. This was a negative mindset that I refused to portray or accept on this journey so I prohibited any negative thoughts on my daily routine.

During the preparation period for my transplant I

received a call from my brother Craig who was a year younger than me. Craig is my very sensitive brother. He was the one who would carefully examine situations or think things through, as children growing up. When one of the farm animals, mostly cows, would die he would become so emotional about the loss. It was no surprise that he was asking about the upcoming treatment and what was involved. Craig asked why I had not considered letting them (my siblings) get tested as possible donors. He was concerned about the possibility of getting a cancer cell since I planned on being my own donor. He said, "Sis I am not trying to tell you what to do, but I just want you to think about letting us be the donor, it makes more sense doing it that way." I actually never thought of it nor did my doctor suggest it for whatever reason. I asked if everyone was okay with this. My mom of course called everyone and reported that they including herself would willingly step up to be there for me. I contacted Dr. Badal and told him what I wanted to do and he pointed me in the direction that I needed to go for the test to take place. I called everyone to inform them that they needed to schedule an appointment with their general doctor for a test to be a bone marrow transplant donor. I also included the address where their blood specimen needed to be sent to at Emory Hospital in Atlanta Georgia.

(Regina's mom and four brothers; Metric top left, Calvin top right Keith bottom left Calvin bottom right, Craig bottom right)

Simple donation may end up saving a life

▶ Blood and bone marrow drive gets under way Wednesday.

By Mary Landers
Savannah Morning News

Regina Thompson lucked out. When chemotherapy failed to cure her cancer, the Savannah mother of two called on her five siblings for a bone marrow transplant.

"My four brothers were a perfect match," said Thompson, 36. "My sister was an almost perfect match."

Only about 30 percent of patients needing a bone marrow match find one in their family. Patients without a family match must look for a match among patients who share a common racial heritage, according to the American Red Cross. Of the 3.4 million persons listed on the bone marrow donor registry, about 270,000 are African Americans.

"For African Americans the likelihood of finding a preliminary match is 59 percent," said Helen Ng of the National Marrow Donor Program. "For Caucasians, it's 85 percent."

The National Marrow Donor Program and the Red Cross are work-

ing to improve those statistics. A blood and bone marrow drive Wednesday is part of that effort and also part of the King Celebration events in Savannah this year.

Placement on the marrow donor registry requires that two small samples of blood are drawn from the donor's arm. The blood is then tested for the donor's particular marrow characteristics. The registry is searched daily for a match. Marrow transplants are used to treat about 70 life-threatening blood diseases,

See **DRIVE**, Page **2C**

Blood and bone marrow drive

When: Wednesday — 6-10 a.m. at the ILA Union Hall, 221 E. Lathrop Ave.; and 2-6 p.m. at the St. Philip AME Church, 613 Martin Luther King Jr. Blvd.

For more information on marrow donations, call the National Marrow Donor Program at 1-800-627-7692 or check out the organization's web site at www.marrow.org

After learning she had lymphoma, Regina Thompson (above) received blood products from her four brothers. When chemotherapy ended and the cancer reappeared, her brother Keith (left, with his son Isiah) donated stem cells — the precursor of all the body's blood cells — to her. Since then, she's been free of the disease.

Life for my family continued to evolve in a positive direction. Meanwhile, a bill came in the mail and I called the insurance company to inquire about the charges. This phone conversation changed my life financially in such a phenomenal way. The insurance representative explained the charges and she then asked how things were going for me. It was beautiful that she took the time to ask how things were going for me. I explained to her that I was prepping for a stem cell transplant. She then went to asking a series of questions which included what hospital I was having the stem cell transplant at, if I was open to receiving information about the different transplant facilities, and why I picked the location to have my transplant. I told the representative that the decision was made basically for my children since they would be able stay in school and their lives would not be uprooted by the events occurring in my life. I asked, "Why was she asking." She advised me that if I chose to have the treatment at a facility that specializes in transplants the insurance company would pay 100% of my medical expenses. If I went to a generalized medical facility they would only pay 80% and I would be responsible for the other 20%. She shared that treatment would easily get up in the two hundred thousand dollar range for my transplant. She also shared that the bone marrow facilities are listed based on the least fatalities to the highest. M.D. Anderson in Houston Texas was one of the top treatment centers at that time. I asked for the information to contact them. I was so excited to learn of this resource. Once my husband was informed of the news, we made a collective decision to call and make an appointment with the facility.

I never thought about calling Dr. Badal to advise him that we made plans to get another opinion about the transplant. Maybe subconsciously I felt like this was my decision and I only needed approval from God and my family. A date was set by the staff at M.D. Anderson and I was instructed by the medical officials to bring all documents and test when I came for the visit.

Chapter 7: DECISIONS- PREPARATION

As the time neared to travel to M.D. Anderson we continue to keep the children informed of the process so they felt a part of all that was going on. The day finally came for the trip to Texas so myself, David and my daughter loaded up the van for that road trip. This long trip was difficult and physically draining for me. While driving through Louisiana, David was stopped for speeding. He was summoned by the officer that stopped us to come to the back of the vehicle. I was reclined back in my seat relaxing when I heard David tell the police officer he was taking is wife to Texas to the cancer center. At that time, I lifted my head up to look towards the back of the van where the activity was taking place. The police officer looked up at me and we locked eyes. He stared at me for a moment and he then turned to David and recommended that he slow down. He also wished us well on our journey. This was the first time my baldness worked in our favor since it got us out of a bind of receiving a speeding ticket.

Once we arrived at M.D. Anderson the staff

informed us that Devida would have to go to the nursery downstairs in the hospital since children were not allowed in that section of the hospital. I thought this was impressive that they provided day care for families with small children. However, at the same time it was scary to be amongst complete strangers and trust them to take care of my six year old. Once Devida laid eyes on the other children in the room she appeared to be comfortable with going into this unfamiliar territory. She said she would be fine with being left in the day care. David and I went upstairs to make the appointment and we met with the doctor who seemed to be nice. After he reviewed my documents and x-rays he agreed with Dr. Badal's diagnoses and the treatment. He made a call to Emory and was given the results of my sibling's tests. He shared that in all his years of practice he never came across a case where all the donors tested were matches. He said my sister was not an exact match but very close. He asked if she had given birth because if so this was the reason she was not a perfect match but still good enough to be a donor if needed. On a side note, he did mention that I must have a special guardian angel looking over me.

Again in this moment there was validation that I was headed down the right road. They agreed to do the transplant while making some points very clear. We were told that this treatment was still experimental. There had been about thirty participants with very few fatalities. The doctor then gave me and David the outline of what I would be agreeing to if we came to that facility for the treatment. They advised us that stem cell is recommended over bone marrow transplant because if the cancer ever came back after having a stem cell transplant I could have another one. Moreover, if I chose the bone marrow transplant I could not do another bone marrow because my body could not handle the trauma again. It was recommended that when choosing my donor I needed to look at which person had the same blood type starting with the youngest sibling. We came to the conclusion that my middle brother Keith would be the optimal choice for my stem cell donor and my older brother Calvin would be my platelet donor. We went back to Savannah to restart preparing the household for this move for my treatment.

In talking with my Mom the decision was made for her to take a leave of absence from her job and relocate to Savannah to take care of the children. We knew we would not have the same amount of money coming into the house hold so we brainstormed on ways to help my mom while staying in Savannah. I went to the local Human Resource Department and applied for benefits. I noticed that the parking lot seemed to have some of the nicest luxury vehicles. When the case worker called me in the back for the interview she told me we would have to liquidate our assets to qualify for stamps. That meant the van and our 401K would need to be cashed in. It did not matter that my family would need transportation to get around in or that I did not have a job. She said that our household did not qualify. When I got home from that visit later that night I received a call from my cousin. She asked how I was coming along. She asked if she could make a suggestion. She wanted to know if the children had to stay in Savannah. She followed that up by saying that Mama would have plenty of help from family members if the children moved to Mississippi. Mama would not have to sacrifice her job and be completely alone in Savannah without any help. She said her spirit lead her to call since she strongly felt having the children around family would help them deal with being away from me the five months I would be in Texas. Again this was one of those moments that just felt right so we talked to the children and they agreed to move with their grandmother while I was in Texas. I went to the schools the next day to find out what was needed to transfer the children to another school in another state. My mother called me with the phone numbers of the schools the children would be attending in Mississippi. I gathered all of the necessary documentation and mailed it to my mom. Then came the task of moving. We were told that once I am released from the hospital out in Texas I would need around the clock care. I called the insurance company to see if they provided funds to help with home health care only to find out that they did not. So I brainstormed on who I could contact to assist with my care once released from the hospital. I called my mother to see if she had any ideas about what family members could help in caring for me. My husband came in the house when I was on the phone discussing this with my mother. After I got off the phone he wanted to know why I was having that conversation with my family. I reminded him that one of the requirements once they release me from the hospital was to have 24 hour care. I explained to him that the insurance does not take care of that expense and therefore I was trying to set a schedule for various family members to come out and help me during the process. David looked at me and said, "Regina that is my job. I have already made arrangements with my job to take a leave of absence to be there for you. The only requirement is that after six weeks I have to return to work for a week in order take the remainder of the leave." I apologized and accepted that I would have my husband at my side. I called my family and told them that I would only need help with one week and my older brother agreed to spend it with me. Now we had the daunting task of finding someone to rent the house because we could not afford to pay rent at two locations during that five month period we would be in Texas.

We talked to a Real Estate company to find a renter. In the meantime, a friend informed us that her brother and his family needed a place to stay and we met with them and they agreed to rent the house. Everything fell in place with little effort. I was then able to focus on preparing to leave my home in the care of renters and to leave my children and friends for five months. In preparation to leave Savannah, I decided to purge my home of anything that was not of God or for those things that I did not need to take into the new life I would return to. I hosted a closet cleaning and freezer/ refrigerator cleaning party with friends. All of my husband's old men magazines went into the trash; clothes I had not worn in a year were either donated or given to a friend. I did the same with the children toys and clothes. What we wanted to keep we stored in our garage in the back of the house. At last, the house was rent ready.

David and I discussed what would happen if there were complications with my transplant and if I did not make it through the treatment. We made the decision to call the pastor of our church and asked for a meeting. Once we met with the pastor, we shared all the events involved in moving the children to Mississippi and that we would be living in Texas for five months until my transplant was complete and I was strong enough to move back home. We explained to our Pastor that M.D. Anderson made it clear that the outcome of the treatment was unknown, but they had to inform us of the positives and negatives of the transplant. The negative factor of this extreme treatment was that it could result in death. We wanted to know from the Reverend if by chance I did not survive my transplant, what David would have to do to have my body transported back to my home church. Our Pastor basically told us he admired that we were having the talk many people refuse to have. We discussed what possible steps that might have to be taken and David even took this opportunity to share with the Pastor his fears which I was not aware of at the time. He told him that some nights he would wake up and just stare at me. He would try to envision his world without me in it; and he couldn't fathom me not being there with him and the children. He shared how he never imagined not having me around to grow old with. I never knew that he had those thoughts. We came to the end of our preparation to leave Savannah. My oncologist called and shared with us that he found out about the change in my plans to have the treatment in Texas. He wanted me to know that he would have done everything possible to help me with the decision to have the Stem Cell Transplant. He wished us well and said he would see me once I got back to Savannah. Lastly, we said our goodbye's to our church friends.

We went to church the last Sunday we had in Savannah. I did not know that David had spoken with the Pastor before service and asked that the church pray for us. At the end of service we were asked to come to the front of the church. This was the most beautiful experience I have ever had since becoming a member of the church. The pastor asked members to come down and pray for my family. At the end of the group prayer the various members came up to hug us and offer their blessings. My pastor's wife walked up and hugged me, she whispered in my ear, "by his stripes you are healed." I had this overwhelming feeling at that very moment that I was truly covered in his blood. I did not know what the next day or year would bring, but I did feel every bit of God's presence and his love for me. I just knew that I would be fine regardless of the outcome.

The next day we took the trip to Mississippi to enroll the children in the Starkville school system and get them settled with my mom. I comfortably gave my mom temporary custody of the children so that she could sign for them in case of emergencies. My Mom's community sponsored cook outs and fish fry's that raised money to help with our relocation to Texas. We got up the next morning and took the children to school. Devida asked that I wear my hat because this was a new school so she did not want to deal with being taunted because of her bald mom. I gladly obliged her since this was not her comfort zone which meant she had to get accustomed to a new environment. We got the children situated, picked up my brother who was chosen to be my donor and headed to Texas to get the process started.

Chapter 8: "HE'S ALWAYS ON TIME"

Once we arrived in Texas, we rented a room, which was not cheap, for the few days we were there. The hospital took my brother through several tests in preparation for harvesting the stem cells from him. David and I met our social worker for the first time and we did everything we needed to do with her which included completing the proper documents. Since the housing at the hospital was out of budget for us, the social worker gave us a list of places in the surrounding area of the hospital and we canvassed the different locations to compare costs. Once again our options were limited due to high cost of living in that medical community. The following day we continued our search while my brother was at the hospital completing the last stages of his testing. Keith called to inform us that he was finished with testing, we picked him up from the hospital and headed back to the room to get packed to leave for the weekend. We briefly talked about the difficulty finding affordable housing, but eventually turned it over to God in prayer to work it out.

Before walking out the door to the hotel, the phone rang and it happened to be from a church located in that medical community. They received our information from the Social Worker and wanted us to know that they could sponsor us with assistance with paying rent. They gave us a list of the places that they represented which we had visited earlier that day. We gladly accepted their offer. When I hung up the phone my brother started to sing an old church hymn, "He Might Not Come When You Want Him, But He's Always on Time". That very moment we surrendered and said we could not be worried about this; that we will work on finding a place when we returned from our weekend in Mississippi, which is when God favor took over.

The drive back to Mississippi was a good drive filled with jokes and laughter. When we returned to my Mom's the children were happy to see us. They were excited about the school and being around cousins. My daughter said one child wanted to know why I had a hat on my head and he asked if I was bald. She said she was snappy with him because he was being ugly. My sister came to visit us at Mom's for the weekend, but we were asleep when they arrived. I heard my niece Sidney's voice in the front of Mom's house the next morning, so I called out to her. When she heard my voice, I could hear her excitement that Auntie Gina was in the house. I could hear her running through the house to get to me because she recognized my voice. When she reached my bedroom door and saw me she immediately stopped in her footsteps. I was sitting on the side of the bed and she seemed puzzled like she did not recognize me, since I was now bald, it was apparent. I kept talking to her to reassure her I was Aunt Gina; my mom came to the door as well to explain to Sidney. She finally realized that it was her aunt because of my voice, but the bald head still confused her. Once she put it all together, she started to laugh. She yelled out to her brother Chris that Auntie was bald and even made the comparison of me being bald like she was when she was a baby. She took steps in the room, but walked very cautiously up to me until she became comfortable with knowing that it was really Auntie Gina.

(A visit from niece Sidney)

The weekend at my mom's was good. I still felt out of sorts, I figured it was because we were coming up on the anniversary of Daddy's death. There seemed to be an elephant in the room during this visit. My mother told me before we headed back to Texas that she trusts that Gods' will would be done, and trust in God. One of my mom's sayings was that "God loaned her children to her and that someday the debt would have to be paid back." Her only prayer is that God takes her before any of her children go home to glory.

We made it back to Texas and moved into what would now be our home for the next few months. My brother and sister-in-law came up a few days later for him to complete the final stages of the transplant preparations. We then returned to the hospital for the itinerary of events preceding my transplant. I was told that the first thing would be changing the catheter that Savannah surgically installed. When I arrived the doctors informed me that they would be changing the port-a-catheter to a central venous line. The doctors preferred working with this type of catheter during stem cell transplants because it performed better less worries of infections. There was an enormous amount of preparation that week which included, testing to determine my cancer status, a bone marrow aspirate, and my brother's preparation for harvesting his stem cells. He was given a medication which was designed to mass produce stem cells into his blood stream. In the days to come this procedure caused a lot of pain in his lower back area. There would be incidents when watching television together and Keith would jump up out of his chair and yell out that his back was killing him. I thought this was just another case of a male not able to handle a little bit of pain. Especially since my brother hates any type of needles or pain for that matter. My brother is the type of person who never meets a stranger. When going for test at the hospital he seemed to catch the attention of the women at the office. One day, my sister-in-law told us she would hurt the women at the office for hitting on her husband. They seemed to have taken a liking to Keith because each time they went for test the nurses would flirt with him. When you meet him you instantly fall in love with him. Since Daddy was a quiet spirit he would always take Keith to places because he could always count on Keith to carry the conversation or engage the crowd so that he would not have to.

The day came to complete the stem cell process with my brother which involved harvesting the stem cell blood from his veins. This was the last step before admitting me to the hospital. My other brothers came up to see me the day I went into the hospital. My sister-in-law voiced the obvious; she said that I looked a little scary and questioned why there were so many tubes connected to my upper chest.   My family sat with me and David for a while in the hospital. We laughed and shared stories. Then the time came for them to leave me. It was apparent by the long goodbyes that they struggled with leaving me because this was all too familiar with the experience with my dad and the many times we visited him at the hospital and left him never knowing if it would be the last time we would see him alive. So I did my best to be as jovial or at least as positive as I could to soothe their pain and worry.

(Regina and David, This was a visit to my mom's to pick my brother up for testing before the transplant. The backpack which I am holding up was attached to my hip at all time. I used it to carry all my medications.)

After things quieted down and it was just me and David, reality struck that the process was finally beginning. The first day of chemotherapy was a success and the following day I was moved to the thirteenth floor. David and I separated before I was moved. The floor on which I would be residing was a donut shape and the nurses' station was in the middle of the floor with the exam rooms situated on the outer perimeter. I was escorted into what I remember being an extremely smaller 6x6 room and I immediately noticed there were two windows on each side of the room. The window on the side of the nurses' station had mechanical arms which were directly above the bed in my room. The arms were in place for the doctor to examine me daily. I learned I would have very little human contact to avoid infections. On the opposite window there was a curtain and the nurse told me that David would be stationed on that side. When the staff drew the curtain David sat there staring in at me. She informed me that we could communicate by phone and explained that this arrangement was for my best interest in order to shield me from possible infections. There was a chair in my room that served as a toilet as well. It consisted of a bowl with a plastic liner and I was to remove and tie it up after each use then place it by the door. The staff would reach in to take it out of my room multiple times during the day.

After the nurse left my room, I went directly over to the phone and signaled for David to pick it up. The first thing that came out of my mouth was this is not going to work. I cannot survive in this setting. He did his best to comfort me and assured me that it was for my safety. I paced the floor in the small space, I tried to sit still, then even tried lying down and nothing seemed to work. I signaled to David again to pick up the phone. I told him that I could not do this; again he tried to comfort me. I called the nurses' station and told them I could not stay in that room. I explained to them that many sacrifices were made to come to Texas, but this one I could not handle. Taking away the one person that I had in Texas with me was not good because I needed my husband by my side. The nurse tried to calm me, but I insisted that she talk with the doctor to find out what other option was available to me and she agreed.

The doctor came to talk to me and reiterated that

upon completion of chemotherapy I would need to be in a safe environment to avoid the possibility of infections which could be fatal. I explained to him that I understood all that, but I needed my husband at close proximity being that he was the only thing I had to hold on to during this part of my treatment. I expressed as best I could that I have to have this to make it through the next few months. After about an hour of going back and forth they agreed to move me to a semi private room. This would allow for David to sleep in the room with me. By the end of that day they moved me to twelfth floor. This was much better for me.

When I woke up the second day, I was itching all over. We discovered that the hair on my entire body had come off during the night and my cloths and the bed was covered with hair. I went to use the bathroom and discovered that the hair in my private covered the lining of my underpants. The only hairs left on my body were my eye brows and lashes. My energy level had weakened tremendously by the end of the second day. Walking to the bathroom was difficult to say the least. Brushing my teeth became a chore for me. There was a chair in the shower stall which I thought was odd in the beginning. It quickly became a much needed and used piece of my furniture in my bathroom. I had to sit just to wash my body because standing required too much energy. My personal hygiene was an absolute must to fight against any germs or infections.

The nurses came in and out of my room so frequently that we knew all of them on a first name basis. They had what looked like an intimidating challenge of changing various bags of chemotherapy, bags of fluid, bags of medication of all sorts and I cannot remember any errors that occurred. They took many tubes of blood daily to see what my levels were. The goal at the beginning was to destroy all the cancer blood cells. During that process not only are the cancer cells destroyed, but the regular/good blood cells are destroyed also because the chemotherapy cannot distinguish between them. Once my counts were dangerously low the nurse came in with a small tube of stem cells, my new blood that my brother gifted to me. She announced that she would be administering the blood and she would sit with me during the transplant for an hour. She was evasive initially, but after I kept inquiring she shared that I could die. This substance was considered foreign to my system and my body could very well reject the new blood. She did explain that if this happened there were medications that they could give me. Try making small talk after that information is revealed. I was tired, so most of the hour was spent in and out of sleep. I made it through the first hour and after that the building stage began.

Chapter 9: RECOVERY- MOTIVATION (CHILDREN/FAMILY)

I assumed that once I received the transplant this miraculous event would occur; that a certain feeling would come over me. When I received my first blood transfusion during my first cancer diagnoses, I remember having this burst of energy. I did not realize how depleted of energy I had become, until I received the new blood. I just assumed I would be up walking around, like I did then but to my surprise the fatigue was still overwhelming. I still felt horrible, struggled most of the time just to walk to the bathroom and I even had problems sleeping at night. Everyday chores required so much energy which I already did not have. While brushing my teeth daily I gagged, when the lunch would be delivered to my room I would gag, and even drinking was difficult. I felt bad all the time and that within itself started to weigh heavy on my mind. I was tired of being tired. I remember being particularly agitated one day. I reached a breaking point and I started to cry hysterically. My husband asked what was wrong and I just explained to him how tired I was, how bad and weak I was feeling which was causing me to want to give up. I remember one day asking God to just let me fall asleep and not wake up. David kept a family portrait in the room by the bedside. One this particular he took the picture in his hand and sat on the side of my bed, he started to say to me that I had to keep the bigger picture in mind. He would point at the family picture periodically and say that the ultimate goal was returning home to our children and that needed to be my only focus. He assured me that he loved me immensely and that he wished he could take away the pain but he was confident that I could do this.

On the days I struggled with being in the state of exhaustion and wanting to give up, he would bring that picture over to the side of my bed and give me this pep talk about fighting harder for the children. That was the exact motivation needed to get me through each day. I started to notice was that there were few phone calls. My mom of course called regularly to check in with me, but none of my siblings called. I simply shrugged it off as their emotions being raw since the loss of our dad. Each day I began to regain strength with the medications prescribed to me. I became restless from being in my small room day after day. One day I asked if I could leave the room for a walk. During this walk, I found out that we actually had a television room on the floor, so when I was allowed to walk the hallway of my floor I would sit in the television room. The first day it was for ten minutes, then twenty, or thirty minutes at a time. I noticed the more I exerted myself the stronger I started to get. My stamina improved daily. Then I heard the doctors say one day I could probably be released from the hospital to our temporary rental apartment. This was all the motivation I needed and I improved and began to walk the hallways multiple times a day, sitting for an hour or more some days. My blood counts continued to improve daily. They kept this posted on a board in my hospital room so that I could see daily my progress which was also motivating for me. With the improvements they started to gradually wean off the intravenous medications to oral medications. Before I knew it, I was taking eighteen pills a day. This was overwhelming in itself, but I did what I had to, in order to be discharged.

It finally happened; the day came when I was released from the hospital. I was given detailed instructions on steps to take since I would not be under their watchful eye. I was permitted to go into the community the more my physical strength improved. A face mask was given to me to wear in public. Certain places were off limits because of the abundance of germs like the movie theaters, cafeterias, and many others locations. Handling fresh fruits, vegetables, or shopping carts was off limits again because so many people touch them when shopping therefore this was extremely dangerous for my immune system. I could only eat cooked foods and nothing raw, no sushi, no fruits nor fresh vegetables.

I came to another phase of my journey. To me this meant I was another step closer to gaining my independence. David and I regrouped and each day we got up early in the morning, took the trip to the hospital for four to five hours of treatments. He sat with me each day without any complaints. He had become accustomed to watching the soap operas each day and it was funny because he started to sound like the retired old people talking to the television telling Mr. Newman from Young and Restless what he needed to do. David would relish in simple delights like eating a Popsicle which was something he never did in our everyday life. He never showed frustration or agitation in taking care of me. I did insist once that I was strong enough for him to at least develop a routine after getting home from the hospital of going somewhere in the community without me like the gym. This brief break I felt helped us grow even stronger as husband and wife. We had at least an hour of being apart, but he was still close enough that if I needed him he was just a call away.

After a while, going back and forth to the hospital started to exhaust me. On this day in particular, I was extremely agitated and my patience was minimal. The nurses visited after each treatment to give me an update on how I was doing physically based on blood tests. But this day it seemed as if they were taking longer than usual to get to me. I started to pace in the treatment room and then went out in the hallway pacing. David tried to calm me, but I felt like the walls were closing in on me. Sleeping at night was so hard and getting up day after day to go get treatment made me feel like things had come to a stall. I made the decision to leave the hospital without seeing the medical staff. David seemed to know not to question me even though he did not agree. When we were exiting the room the nurses approached us and I apparently had a look of anxiety on my face and they asked what was wrong. There was a chair outside the room and I just collapsed in it. They helped get me back into the room and started to probe me, trying to understand what was going on. I started to cry uncontrollably and I said to them that coming to the hospital daily was a challenge. One nurse said okay we wanted to tell you that instead of every day during the week you can now come every other day. That still did not help so again they asked me what was really wrong. I paused and simply replied, "I have not seen my children in more than a month, and although I speak to them often over the phone I still have not seen their lovely faces and I miss them so much. I need to see them." The other nurse said that's not a problem, we will have a young lady call you later today. She will visit you at your apartment to give you and David a phone that will not only allow you to talk to the children, but to see them simultaneously while talking. The world lifted off my shoulders when she said that. I suddenly felt like a little child anxious to get this new toy. I was then told to make an appointment to see the hospital's psychologist to discuss my thoughts and feelings.

Later that day, we received a call and agreed to meet with the representative the next day for the device. We also made an appointment for the hospital's psychologist. The following day we met with Ms. Sherrie, the psychologist, and I found it hard in the beginning to share my feelings with this complete stranger. After preliminary questions about my thought process, I finally opened up to her. I told her that I was so confused since there were so many thoughts inside me that I did not know how to deal with what was bottled up. I shared with her the past events of losing my dad to cancer and never really having time or the right opportunity to grieve. I told her about my problems sleeping, but I refused to take sleeping pills because the dangers of becoming addicted. Ms. Sherrie told me in simplest terms that all I had to do was express my emotions, talk about what I was feeling just like I was doing in our session. She shared with me the key is releasing the feelings not internalizing them. She talked about the dangers of stress on the mind and body and I immediately knew that a lot of my suffering was stress induced. It has been found that many people struggle with talking about their feelings not understanding that this is actually therapy for them and as a result they suffer. Some people even after being advised to share their emotions find it too difficult to and instead they never do and this creates a life of pain and suffering. She said "talking is all you have to do Regina." She also shared some techniques of relaxation, guided imagery, listening to tapes of the ocean or the crickets chirping and frogs singing in the night. She gave us tapes to take home to experiment with for solutions to my sleeping issues. David seemed to submit to the tapes because he was able to fall asleep without hassle. I enjoyed the sounds, especially the waves crashing in the ocean, but still I struggled with falling asleep.

We also met with the young lady who operates a non-profit organization that helps individuals who are patients at M.D. Anderson. Her organization assists people with needs they might have like food assistance, utility assistance, etc. She provided us with a telephone that had a monitor attached and told us that she would be sending one to my mother's home as well. The way it works is once you call one another and connect you can see each other while talking on the phone. She entrusted us to this device for two weeks so that I could have that moment of seeing my children because my heart just craved to see their little faces. We were extremely appreciative for the help that her organization was willing to give to make sure my stress levels were manageable. My mother called as soon as they received the phone in Mississippi. This was our first reunion since leaving them months ago. Mama, my daughter and son looked as if they were crunched together to make sure they were able to see me. Mama immediately said, "Look at my bald headed baby." Before she could complete the sentence my daughter said, "It does not matter, my mommy is so beautiful." My son being at the delegate age of transitioning into puberty just simply said, "hey ma." Tears rolled down my face and I was filled with so much joy. The children talked about their new schools and how they enjoyed being around an abundance of family members. In Savannah they did not have any family around so this was pure joy for them to have this opportunity. Wrapped in that moment and seeing their faces made all the difference in the world for me. This was the motivation I needed to get through the next phase of my treatment. I started to devise a plan to return back home to my children.

When we went to the hospital for my treatments, David would drop me off at the front door because the parking lot was a long distance from the hospital. I would wait for him and we would take the elevator to my appointment. I told David that we needed to get up a little earlier in the mornings and instead of him dropping me off we would walk from the parking garage, walk up a few flight of stairs to the appointment. Once finished with my treatments again we would walk back to the garage. I would take the elevator to the car because by that time I would be exhausted.

Thanksgiving was soon upon us and my family wanted to visit. I talked to my doctor and he stressed that I could not be around any one with fevers, colds or any kind of infections. I gave my family the permission to come visit.

The children were told they had to practice washing their hands before coming around me. They of course did what was needed to be around mom. My sister-in-law was excited to share some of her new side dishes with that she was preparing for dinner. Unfortunately, I was unable to eat them because the ingredients in the salads were off limits. All my foods had to be cooked I told her. She understood and I explained that I would have plenty of time once everything was over to indulge in her new recipes. Thanksgiving was great even though I was not able to eat much. Just being around family was all I needed for that extra boost of motivation. We all had a hard time saying goodbye at the end of the visit. After my family left, I started plotting in my head what my next move would be.

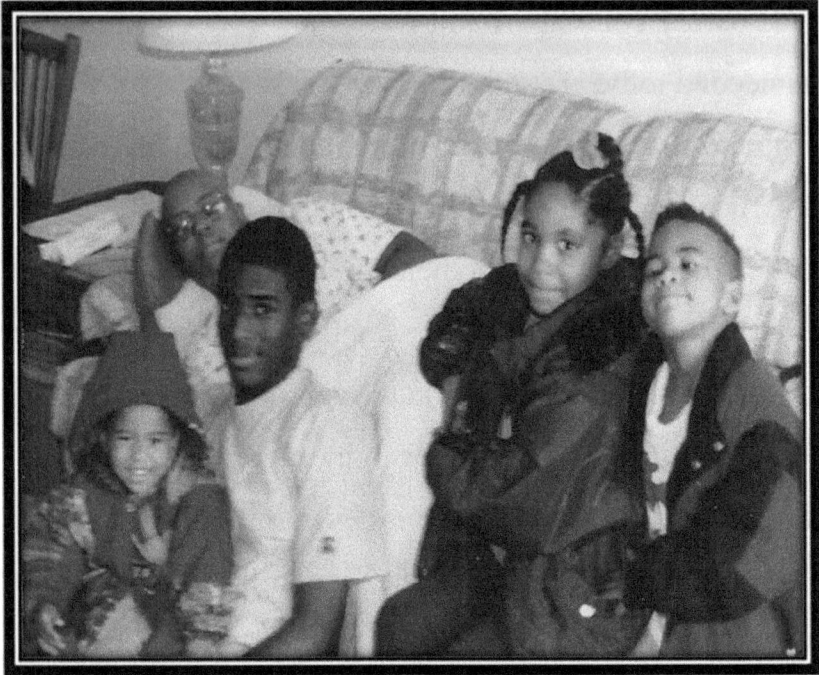

(This picture took place Thanksgiving in Houston Texas. (left to right, Sidney my niece, Jeremiah, my son, Devida, my daughter, Christopher, my nephew, and myself Regina on the sofa)

At one of my treatments I was told I was not drinking enough fluids so I had to go home with containers of fluid connected to my port a catheter to avoid any problems. I continued to regain more and more strength; therefore I decided to increase my workouts. We started walking in the evenings around the apartment complex. I noticed that I was able to get some rest during the night with the walking. Eventually, we started to venture out into the Houston Texas community a little more because my stamina improved with each day. We would stop at little shops that did not seem to have very many people. I would go grocery shopping with David. He would prepare all the meals, but a lot of the times he had to ask for directions on cooking because this was a task he did very little of back home in Savannah. In fact I told him once we returned he would have to take on some of that responsibility since he was mastering the job of cooking in Texas. Sometimes he would ask repeatedly how to prepare a dish that it became exhausting constantly explaining to him how to prepare things. I sometimes threatened to get up myself and do the cooking for him because of the many questions he had. But he would always come through, although some days in the kitchen were more prolonged than other days.

Chapter 10: "BY HIS STRIPES"

Maneuvering throughout the community was quite comfortable for me as a bald person because that is all you saw around the city of Houston. I started leaving my hats at home, unless the weather was too cool. When at home in Savannah, I did not like how people stared even when I was wearing a headpiece. For some reason, cancer patient experiences a change in skin which causes their skin to turn have an ashy and pale appearance and that alone catches one's eye. Instead of them asking what is wrong they just stare. So it felt comfortable as a bald person being in the medical community in Houston and that was alright with me. The time drew near when David had to return for work in Savannah for a week to avoid losing his job. We called my older brother for assistance. While he was down for the week caring for me he donated more platelets. He molded very nicely into the position of care giver. Each morning he would go to the gym and go for his runs to remain in shape for the military. One night for dinner he wanted my scalloped potatoes so he asked for my recipe. I coached him through the process and watched carefully while he prepared them. He actually did a great job from the little I was able to stomach down but he on other hand ate every bit of them.

One morning when I got up to get dressed, while brushing my teeth, I noticed blood in my fingernails on both hands. I looked at my arms but could not find anything. I did not look up in the mirror of the bathroom, but I went back to the bed and noticed that the sheets had blood on them close to my pillow. I looked in the mirror and that is when I noticed my shirt was bloody. I believe I had began to hyperventilate; I had to calm myself because my brother was still at the gym and I knew that I had to have myself cleaned up before he came in or this would freak him out. I called the hospital and explained what I found and was told to come in immediately because apparently my catheter broke and I bled out overnight. So once my brother came in I told him the hospital needed me there immediately for some test and that his shower had to wait. He of course asked if anything was wrong and I assured him I was okay. Once we made it to the hospital they performed the procedure to correct the broken catheter which took a good amount of time. Once everything was finished, I explained to Calvin what actually happened and his eyes grew so big but we were both happy everything was okay. David soon made it back and relieved my brother. We thanked him for the huge sacrifice he made for us. He of course said he did not have to sacrifice anything; I was his sister and whatever or whenever I needed him he would always be there for me.

Christmas was approaching and we had to wrap our brains around the notion that we would not be able to purchase the children any gifts for Christmas. We just trusted God to make the occasion a joyous one for the family. My sister and her husband came down to visit for a few days. They did a little Christmas shopping while they were visiting. I was not able to walk around the toy store for long so I sat at the front of the store for most of the shopping experience. After they left I asked my doctor if I could go visit my family for the Christmas holiday. I assured him I was strong enough to handle the drive and that we would only be gone three days at most. He was not too crazy about this, but he eventually gave in and stressed the importance of the detailed instructions I needed to follow while home. He asked that it only be my mom and the children, not to go if anyone was sick. He emphasized not to have other guests visit because too much interaction with multiple people touching and hugging I could become ill. We called ahead to inform Mama of all the doctor's orders and she promised she would not tell anybody of our visit.

Once we arrived to my mom's house we were greeted with much love from the children. Mama had us to put the car in the back of the house so people passing would not notice and be tempted to come see us. Shortly after being home a delivery came to my mom's home with all these boxes filled with Christmas presents. My good friend from my old job apparently raised money and went out shopping to purchase my children gifts for Christmas. We were shocked; over joyed, grateful, every emotion you can imagine was experienced. I believe this was the first Christmas my children had more toys than any Christmas they have ever experienced. My friend shared with me she finally gained the understanding of the frustration I would have when trying to find African American dolls for my daughter because she had a hard time finding them. For the entire weekend, people came in and out of the home visiting my mom and the children. David did his best to keep them from getting too close, but of course they had to lay eyes on me and express their love and joy to see us. At one point David asked that I not come in the front of the house because so many people were visiting. Mom insisted that she did not tell a soul which everyone confirmed, they just wanted to bring a gift to the house for the children and mom. The children had a wonderful time, but once again we had to depart for Texas.

Immediately after returning, I developed a fever. I was admitted to the hospital and was so sick. The symptoms came up on me so quickly that it was frightening. After a few days in the hospital I was released and the doctor again explained to me that it is going to take time for my system to get stronger. I would have up to a year before my body would be able to fight off infections on its own. When the holidays ended, the doctor said I had two more months to be released and I told him that my goal was to narrow that down to one month. He agreed that I was doing extraordinarily well. I told David that I was so over Texas. Home is where I wanted to be.

The hospital was lessening the amount of pills needed. I would receive intravenously immunoglobulin treatments which are designed to empower the body's immune system to fight infections. My fluid intake was good. The test showed no signs of cancer and I was feeling good. Fatigue was still a huge part of my daily routine. Since I knew that my energy level was better in the mornings, we explored the community during this time and the evenings were spent lounging around in the apartment. David had his routine of going to the gym in our apartment complex to give us an hour or more to escape from each other. He even ventured out into the community to check out the local pawn shops like he did back at home when he felt I needed more time alone or he needed more time to himself. That was usually during that menstrual time, even though I was not experiencing this now the symptoms still came each month. He would never be too far away, just in case I needed him. With each day my strength and stamina improved.

Once again, the time came to take x-rays and various tests to monitor my recovery process. The day came to take the dreaded bone aspirate test. I dreaded this test because of the pain. David and I were at the hospital sitting in the waiting room to be called back for this test, but the longer it took the more anxious I became. When I am nervous, if I'm sitting down, my right leg shakes uncontrollably. My husband noticed and asked what the problem was since I had that test before. Before I could explain they called me back. The nurse told me that David could not be in the exam room. I told her if I had to do the test he had to be with me. She assured me that they would give me something to help relax me, but again I told her I needed my husband. She reluctantly allowed him to come back with me. I was given instructions to get onto the table and position my body in preparation for the test. I looked at my husband with tears in my eyes and asked him to hold my hand. The nurse gave me a local anesthesia to calm me and shortly after that I announced that I had to throw up. David handed me a small basin and I released everything in my stomach. Once I finished the nurse asked why I was so worked up, but by then I could hardly speak from crying so much. The grip I had on David's hand intensified. The doctor carried on with the procedure and my husband whispered every move the doctor was making. He said they made a small incision in my skin, and then they inserted an object that looked like an ice pick into the top part of my left hip at the pelvic bone area. I heard the doctor say I would feel pressure because he was creating an opening in the bone. He followed that by saying we are in now and we are drawing out a sample of your marrow so you will feel a slight pressure again. This felt like something was being drawn out of my hip.

After everything was over they bandaged me up and we went home. I was sore for a couple of days, but quickly healed from the procedure. The various tests yielded clear readings and I was officially told that my cancer was in remission. He made it clear that there is no cure for cancer only treatments for cancer. Remission only implies that there is no evidence, signs or symptoms of the cancer. But there is always a chance that the tests cannot pick up on a small indicator that the cancer remains. I immediately asked my doctor if he would allow me to leave earlier than my original scheduled time. He finally agreed and we prepared to leave Houston Texas at last. My last visit to the hospital involved them removing my intravenous catheter. All of the staff in that department made me feel so good. We were told that in-spite of all that we encountered and endured we did exceptionally well. We were given detailed instructions about after care with my oncologist in Savannah. Emphasis was put on precautionary measures to take over the next year which included, not going into crowded places to avoid germs, staying out of the sun, not entering swimming pools, lakes, rivers, not eating fresh fruits and vegetables only cooked foods and not taking vaccines (live virus) because my body could not fight off the virus. The staff at the hospital wished us well. We were told that every three months I would need to have the various tests and x-rays to test for any signs of the cancer. We were asked to come back yearly for exams at the hospital.

Happy about the news, we called home and told mom we were on the way and not to tell the children so that we could surprise them. We said our goodbyes to Houston and all the individuals who assisted us in our journey while at M.D. Anderson. We gave God all the glory for the experience and for his grace and mercy. I was reminded of the hug and words I received from the first lady of my church when she sent me off to Texas months ago, Isaiah 53:4-5, "By his stripes we are healed." I finally understood that this did not mean a gift of physical healing, but a gift of spiritual healing. I placed my faith and trust in God and was at peace with however my Savior answered my prayer for healing, be that a physical healing in heaven or physical healing here on earth. This journey of discovering myself helped me see that I had to change me in order to heal. Amen.

Once we returned to my mother's, the children were elated to see us. They were eager to share how wonderful it was living in Mississippi with family. In fact Jerry and Devida wanted us to consider moving to Mississippi. Devida said it would be easy since they were already in school and we would not have to worry about enrolling all over again, therefore all that was left was to sell the house in Savannah. She went as far to say that we could all live with grandma until we could find another house. Jeremiah was on the fence with the notion because he had friends back in Savannah, but whatever we did he said it would be fine with him. We made the decision to let the children stay the remainder of the year with my mother since I was still not strong enough to presume my role as full time parent and David needed the help. We stayed a few days with the children and then drove back to our home in Savannah.

When we walked into our home after being gone for four months the first thing I noticed was the odor of the house. Not that it smelled bad, but it no longer had my families' scent in it. The house looked the same but did not smell like our home. The couple who rented it from us during that time took good care of it for us and we were so grateful for that. We were extremely eager to get our vibe back in our home. The first thing we did was strip all the bed linens and mattress covers, clean the bathrooms, mop the floors, vacuum the carpet, clean out the refrigerators and that alone helped relax our minds. David did most of the work, but I helped out as much as my energy level would allow. Eventually things came together in a few days and the walls and things started to smell like us again.

We quickly resumed our routine which consisted of David going back to work. I reunited with my oncologist and continued by weekly immunoglobulin treatments at the hospital. We both started to make walking in our neighborhood a routine at least when the weather permitted. During the times I would be home alone, I would take time to meditate, pray, and reflect on all that had transpired over the last year with my health and daddy's death. I discovered that I was actually upset with my dad because I felt like he gave up on life. He took on this stance to close himself off from the world not allowing any one to come visit the house because he felt that people did not really care about him they only wanted to see what the disease had done to him. I can recall someone saying that one of my sister-in-laws commented that we showed very little emotion at my dad's funeral implying that we were damaged people. Those events kept playing over and over in my head what and how could we have saved him from leaving us so soon.

One day when out for a walk, during my daily prayer I remember an overwhelming feeling that came over me about my questions to God asking why he took daddy so soon. This dream filled me with a calming feeling that daddy did not give up on life, he gave cancer all he knew and that did not mean he gave up nor did it mean he handled his situation in a wrong way. He had developed a great relationship with God long before he became ill and it was just his time to go. Nothing could have been done differently for him to still be here with us. He shared with me before he died that I was more like my mom, I had a little more fighting spirit in me. He also said that as individuals we all have our own personal coping mechanism to stuff life brings us and just because his looks differently from mine does not make how he does it wrong. He assured me then that he was going to be okay. I finally was at peace with my father's death. I then began to reflect on the wonderful times we had together when he was here. I would think about the hour long conversations we had after he gave his life over to God and that made it more tolerable. I still missed him and would have days of crying, but I found solace in the fact that he was no longer suffering from Cancer, he was finally at peace. So as far as what my sister-in-law felt did not matter what so ever.

During the time the children were away, I took on hobbies that helped relax my mind and spirit. I knew that stress was not my best friend so crafts became something that allowed me to completely relax when my mind was cluttered. I remember one day I was working with a piece of clay to form an African mask and after I finished this task it dawned on me that my brain was so relaxed. In that moment I thought of nothing else except for that clay; the bills, children, cancer, and medical appointments, none of that entered my brain. What was even more enlightening was that when I did focus back on those aspects of my life there was clarity and it was awesome. This even helped me sleep better at night. The end of the summer quickly approached and we had to go pick up the children. David and I decided before traveling back to Mississippi for the children to do a special dinner for our family members who participated with saving my life on this journey with cancer. A friend from high school sent me this framed poem right after my father died that seemed to fit all that my family had gone through over the past several months which read:

You know,
I've been thinking about your circumstances
and wondering why
it is that we sometimes have
to go through times like this.
I was reminded of the way
grapevines have to be pruned back...
Sometimes the pruning
seems so severe
that you wonder how
the vines will ever recover.
But it's only because
of those prunings that the roots
receive the strength
they need to grow deep and strong.
When the vines recover,
they bear even more fruit
and have the added strength
to withstand storms and droughts.
-Author unknown

I decided to give this poem to my siblings. I wanted them to know that we would be okay. Although, Daddy would be missed tremendously, I was on the road to a great recovery and that this experience made us so very strong. I stressed the importance of having that personal relationship with God, having faith and trusting that whatever the outcome of the situation, we would be still be okay. I expressed my gratitude and love for everyone who participated in the success of my transplant. David and I expressed to our children just how proud we were of them excelling in school during this difficult time. We especially wanted them to see that it truly takes a village not just to rear children, but to help each other get through obstacles life confronts us with. For my husband, I played this song by a Canadian artist, "Because You Loved Me." He honored our vows and I wanted to honor him in this moment with family and friends. I thanked my family and my children for all they did for me during this time. While the things I shared with my family at this dinner were just words, I did my best to convey to them that they gave me the reason to fight for one more day just to be with them. Like the song says "when I couldn't do for myself they were there to keep me lifted". They gave me faith because they believed in me. I shared with them that I was still standing because of their love for me. Love prevailed on this journey with cancer. What could I say to my mother other than thank you so much for your prayers, your faith, your words of comfort, your help, the prayer line you created for me around the world, and for being my back bone when mine was shaken. I thanked God over and over again for his love and for my family.

When it was time to go home, the children had a difficult time saying goodbye to my mom. They cried and literally begged for us to move to Mississippi. We were able to calm them and we reminded them that we would all be okay be that in Mississippi or Georgia. I told them that they would still have their summers with grandma. The drive back home was bittersweet. The children were excited to see their friends again, but they missed their grandmother whom they had the luxury of being with for the past twelve months of their life.

Chapter 11: For Better or Worse

Once we were back in Savannah we helped the children get readjusted and settled back into the routine of being back home. They had no trouble getting acclimated to their lives in Georgia. They started school and meshed back into activities that comforted them. I came up on my first round of checkups to see if the cancer was still in remission. The ladies in x-ray department, like always, were delighted to see us. They were elated to know that I was a success story because they understood first-hand the extent of my condition. They labeled me the poster child for cancer. They told me that David and I had such a positive outlook and great spirit during this walk and that was impressive to them. They see so many people and personalities, and it was refreshing for them to see a couple like David and I, who always came through their doors with a smile and encouraging words for other people. They shared with us that they prayed for our family. It was enlightening to hear that people you would never think would take out the time to send up prayers for you.

After my x-ray results yielded good results the doctor wanted to do a bone marrow aspirate. I told Dr. Badal that if he could not put me to sleep, I would rather not take it. I expressed to him that I felt good and the blood test and x-rays did not show any signs of cancer so I did not see the need. He did not hassle me and further about having it done, but would ask each time I was to have all the checkups again. During a visit with Dr. Badal, he informed me that M.D. Anderson hospital kept writing him about not receiving any results of bone marrow test that were supposed to be done yearly. He told the staff at M.D. Anderson politely told them that he could not force now convince me to take the test and therefore not having the results was okay.

After about six months of being back home, I started to see some changes in David's willingness to participate with my recovery. When I would ask him to go walking with me I was told he did not like walking he only liked running. He said that he only walked with me to help me during that time and he felt like I could now do those things on my own. After the cancer I started to have various side illnesses that seemed to pop up from time to time. The cancer experience induced menopausal symptoms that I was not prepared for. Whenever I would try to discuss the circumstances he remained very disinterested. It was always the same answers whenever I asked for help or even tried to discuss what was happening. It appeared that he was exhausted with being my caregiver and that he no longer wanted that role or position. This brought on un-welcomed feelings of abandonment for me. My caring and devoted husband who was constantly there for me was now treating me like I had a plague. He came in later and later from work and had no problems justifying his lack of interest in the activities which I partook in.

About a year of being out of the transplant, I was working out at the gym and started to notice my energy level drastically dropping. Even my personal trainer thought I was just trying to get out of doing work outs. Then my finger nails and toe nails at the base turned black. My mouth seemed to have blistered; the area underneath my eyes had turned black, my underarms darkened as well as under my breast. Following up with my doctor to try and find out what was happening was vital. I had to again have different tests to see what was occurring with my body. I did start to feel a little better about a week after it started. The holidays were approaching and we made plans to visit my mom.

We took the trip to Mississippi with the children. My mother like always assigned me to cooking Christmas dinner. That Christmas morning when I awoke, I entered the kitchen and quickly noticed I was not feeling very well. I told my mom that I was going back to lie down for about an hour or so and I would then get dinner started. She checked in on me about thirty minutes later and my health had quickly declined. I started to run a fever so David brought me medication to stop the fever. About an hour later my fever went from 101 to 103.8 and David demanded to take me to the hospital because they said I started to talk out of my head. This frightened the both of us so he called to Houston Texas once we got to the hospital emergency room. The staff advised us before we left Texas, which was now about a year ago, that in any emergency situation to call. It was made clear that I could not just take any medication as a result of having a compromised immune system. The medical staff out at

Texas did collaborate with the emergency room staff in Mississippi on what to actually do for me. Once my fever broke, I started to feel better and was more coherent. The staff in the emergency room informed me that David was diligent about communicating with the medical staff in Houston, Texas. He did not want them to give me medication that would hurt me more than help me. One of the nurses said to me that I had a special man on my hands.

We left the hospital and went back to my mom's house a couple of hours later. Although I didn't have a fever my energy level still seemed to be very poor. I spent the day in bed and my siblings that came for dinner would come into the bedroom to look in on me. My brother who donated the stem cells was the only person who asked why my eyes looked like someone had given me two black eyes. I had not a clue what was going on with me. We got through that visit with my mom and once I was strong enough to travel we went back to Savannah. Upon our return, I went to see Dr. Badal and he started me again with the immunoglobulin treatments. Later on after various tests it showed that I developed Graft vs. Host

Disease (GVHD). It was explained to me that this is when the donor's (Keith my brother) immune cells mistakenly attack the recipient's normal cells. So all the symptoms I was experiencing indicated this was a chronic form of the disease. I later discovered this could have been fatal because my symptoms were the severe form. Again we got through this experience and David was a trooper the whole time.

After things calmed back down, I decided to talk to David about why he seemed to be pulling away from me. I was confused about what was happening, now that things were improving with my health it appeared that he was becoming less enthusiastic or less interested. I needed to understand why he came to my side in extreme cases of health problems, but outside of that it seemed as if he was not there for me. He told me that he was tired, that he was burned out as a caregiver. He wanted me to take over with things he felt I could handle on my own. He emphasized that it did not mean he didn't love me, but instead he wanted me to stand on my own two feet. I expressed to him that you never place limitations on how much you can give a person in need. Although I did understand through personal experiences that as adults we get tired in general with things, people, and yes even with our children sometimes. We would never make the children feel as though they were just too much to handle or that they were a burden. His choice of words in explaining his feelings were hurtful. I never thought that he could be tired and needed to regain his own personal space. When I struggle with understanding a situation I retreat to what centers me and that is prayer. My visits to the park to take long walks and have intimate conversations with God always helps me to clear my mind. That process off strengthening my body helps with strengthening my mind and spirit. David and I got through this and he vowed to communicate his feelings in a more delicate manner. I realized that I had made my husband my crutch, my soft place to land. I was blessed to have a wonderful man who stood beside me on this journey. He never complained but had the foresight to see the need for me to regain my independence and he pushed me in that direction not to hurt me but help me. I was reluctant and afraid of getting back into the world but he knew that it was important for my recovery. This was the end of our cancer journey and the beginning of the rest of our lives post victory of lymphoma twice.

A Journey Glimpse: From Family and Friends

This section highlights Regina Thompson's experience from the standpoint of her family and a friend. Often times the supporting relatives and friends of the loved one with cancer go through a challenging time as well and their stories are forgotten. The brief accounts below are snapshots of the feelings and the experiences in their own words.

From Regina's Mom:

A knot developed on her neck. Regina started having problems and the following Monday after Mother's Day. She went to the doctor who said she had cancer with six months to year to live. I gained my composure and prayed for strength. I thought to myself God does not give doctors power to put time on my daughter's life. I lost it when I got off the phone. I prayed, "Jesus you made Regina and you know about her inside and out and I will put it in your hands; I know you will heal her; man doesn't have that power." I questioned my faith...where was my faith. I had a feeling inside she would be okay, but the word CANCER was harsh. The hardest part to deal with was not being able to visit since Melvin was going through the same situation, with different circumstances.   The first month was the hardest because dealing with two people battling cancer was a challenge. With Melvin being so sick he had to stay in the hospital for three months. When my husband sent Regina home to rest, he had a talk with the doctor and said, "I am a church man and I am not afraid to die. I've prayed for the Lord to take me and spare **my** daughter. Baby I love you so much, but Regina needs to raise her children." A cool and calm feeling came over me. The night before he passed he gave me a long talk and accepted losing the battle to cancer. He talked to our older child Calvin, explaining to him to make funeral arrangements and not let me do anything regarding the funeral arrangements. "Bury me military style", he requested. Regina was crying so hard, he told her to quit that crying and encouraged her to be strong like her mother.

I was given custody of Jeremiah and Devida. David said, "You take care of my children and I will take care of your daughter." We would often video in with

Regina during her time spent in Indiana and Texas for transplant." Everything the doctor said she had to complete she completed it sooner than doctors expected. I believe it was God showing her how he works. When it came time to choose donors she chose Keith, who is also terrified of needles. She chose the scariest one of the bunch, but Regina and Keith are very close. He said he would give his life for Regina. Cancer…I really did not know how to deal with it or how it damaged the body. I joined a group where we had conversations about cancer how it worked and learned about the different types of cancer. Everybody was connected with cancer in some way whether they knew someone with cancer, they were patients themselves, or knew people that lost the battle to cancer. One thing I know now, you have to be able to talk about it because if not, it will destroy you. They said cancer wasn't going to kill my husband but a heart attack would since he wouldn't talk about it. My husband lost his brother, two aunts, and cousins, to cancer. At the time my husband was battling cancer, my brother moved from Ohio with cancer as well.

My relationship with Regina is so close that we are

almost like sisters. My husband used to tell her, "you don't rule this house." She calls to talk 3-4 four times a day. We have become even closer since cancer surfaced in our lives. Regina is strong headed, kind hearted, worries about when people don't react in a certain way; soft-hearted, helping hand; we are so much alike.

From David (husband):

The scariest event was the Monday following Mother's Day in 1995, which is the day Regina was diagnosed with lymphoma. What made it so frightening was what I did not know. I recall Dr. Pope telling us that Regina had non-Hodgkin lymphoma, and one of us asking what non-Hodgkin lymphoma is and Dr. Pope replying cancer and telling us to go directly to the hospital that we had just left. The urgency and the word cancer candidly frighten me. I can truly say that Regina's commitment to raising Jeremiah and Devida and her faith are what allowed her to endure the process of the transplant. There came a time when we felt a calm confidence that God had everything under control that our mission was to seek the next step.

I can't distinguish a particular time when I had to be most supportive. I just recall knowing that every day I had to be my most compassionate, upbeat, and confident self regardless of what was going on within. The best description of our relationship is that it's a love that is evolving, committed and determined to win. I have learned that cancer either directly or indirectly, is a day away from each of us, that it is not a bigot, it truly does not care who you are or what you have. Cancer claimed the life of my college roommate as he was preparing to conquer the world just as it did Steve Jobs as he was seemingly on top of the world. You can be the best of men, committed to your church, your family, your country, your community, revered by all those around you and cancer will overlook all of that as it did in September 1996 when it claimed the life of my father in law.

A positive outlook, strong will, and a willingness to share not hide are common characteristics of my wife Regina, my sister Virginia, our dearest friend Quila and countless others who have survived.

From Jeremiah Thompson (Regina's son):

The scariest event had to be not knowing what was going to happen to my mother and where Devida and I would go if things didn't work out. There was a 50/50 chance whether she lived or died, and it was terrifying because each day I woke up I did not know if the night prior was my last time talking to her. Then I wasn't sure if David was going to split Devida and me up if things turned for the worse. I know for a fact that my mother surrounding herself with nothing but positive people is what helped her survive. She did not allow any negative thoughts into her mind, she did not allow any negative people to be in her presence and she would not allow any negative people to be around the family. This alone made her stronger and placed her in a mental state that allowed her to receive her blessings and to be healed.

I had to be most supportive through the entire process for my mother, sister and grandmother. We had just watched my grandfather suffer in the past of the same exact cancer that my mother had and it was very rough times. My mother needed to know that my sister and I were safe and sound and still living our lives as if nothing was wrong. I had to be there for my grandmother as she was trying to make sure my sister and I had everything we needed and on the other hand trying not to show any stress of worrying about her daughter who was miles and miles away. In a sense, I had to be a big brother, son, a husband, and grandson. Before the cancer situation my mother and I did not have the best relationship. She would speak when I came home from school, but we never went in depth of how my day was or about the activities I was involved in. Post cancer I can tell that she looked at life totally different. She was more energetic, more friendly, and more engaged and involved in my life. She and I are best of friends now and we literally talk every single day. I feel weird if we skip a day without communication and I feel weird if she is not asking me a hundred million questions about my life. Some may think that we are too close, but who cares I only have one mother and I will be as close as I want to be with her!

Since this whole ordeal, I have learned a lot about cancer. It has taken a lot of my family and most importantly it is a very serious disease that affects more people than you actually realize. It has the power to take a life as well as the power to bring lives closer together. You only get one life to live so please take care of it.

When one hears the word cancer people tend to be frightened and afraid. Do the research and get tested, because the sooner you know about it the better chance that you may have to be on the winning side of this serious battle.

From Devida Thompson (Regina's daughter);

The overall experience was scary, but the scariest moment for me as a young girl was when my mother came to visit me and my brother at our grandmother's house and due to her weakened immune system she became ill. It scared me because I felt as though I was responsible for her getting sick and I was terrified for her well-being. It is a scary situation being young and not fully understanding that the tiniest thing could trigger illness in your mother. Throughout this experience, my mother had a strong will to live and as a mother with two young children, she knew she wasn't ready to leave her family behind. She knew that my family; my brother, my father and myself, weren't ready to live a life without her. I credit my mommy for not only fighting for her life but for fighting for her family.

I was very young when my mother was diagnosed with cancer so I wasn't very aware of how much support I gave, but I do remember the night my mother began to lose her hair. She came out of the bathroom with a very concerned face and her and my Dad stood in the mirror talking. I told my mother that she was just as beautiful with no hair as she was with a head full of hair; I sincerely meant every word.

I have a very strong relationship with my mother. She is the closest person to me. As I have gotten older my relationship with my mother has blossomed. To describe our relationship I would have to say it is one of those loving friendships with the understanding that she is the mother and I am the daughter.

From Calvin (oldest brother; platelet donor):

The scariest event for me was when I received the phone call from her and she told me she had cancer; my first thought was that I would lose my little sister. I believe that being a tight family helped my sister; we all pulled together to help her get through this experience. My most supportive role was when I went to Houston to stay with her while David returned to work in Ga. I left my army station at Fort Hood to assist for a while where I cleaned, cooked, and took her to appointments. Regina and I are more than just sister and brother we are best friends we have been through a lot together and I will leave it at that.

What I have learned about the big "C" word is that it can be beaten, my sister is living proof of that. Also you MUST trust in God and be a family that prays together and all will be worked out.

From Craig (third oldest sibling):

The scariest moment for me was when I first found out that she was diagnosed with cancer. That moment was so surreal to me almost like being in a dream and there was so much disbelief. I didn't know how to support her at the time or what I had to offer her that would even matter. All I had at that moment to offer her was my strength in adversity. I often wanted to cry, but instead I showed her the strong side of me hoping in some way it would give her strength. Now sometimes I find myself sitting and waiting to receive bad news as it related to my sister, don't know why it just pops in my head unexpectedly.

If asked what qualities Regina had to make it through; it would be easy to answer, strength and faith. I often asked myself, if it was me what I would do? And quite frankly I would have just given up. I completely admire my sister's faith, not only in herself, but also in God. You have to understand the dynamics of our family to get a true picture of how much we endured just for being Melvin Thompson's children. There were those who'd rather see her fail and die rather conquer the disease. Regina's strength still to this day overwhelms people who come in contact with her. I think it's because we live a doomsday world therefore we expect everyone to have a "give up" attitude.

When my sister was in Houston in the cancer ward, I felt most supportive to her. I had friends who prayed for my sister because of their friendship and love for me. I tried to visit her as often as I could in those most difficult times to somehow just let her know that I loved her with all my heart and soul. I didn't have much faith at the time that she would beat this thing called cancer, but because of her strength and faith she made a believer out of me that if anyone could beat this disease it would be her.

Our relationship has always been strong. We are similar in a lot of ways, most of all our independence. We share stubbornness like no other and we are both self-sufficient. There was a time in my life when I resented my sister's behavior because of a certain boyfriend she had at the time. I think it was the fact that my expectations of her were rather high and I could not understand how she could be so blinded by this guy. It wasn't until after I went to junior college that I realized how my sister impacted so many others with her kindness and many loved her. People were quick to offer me their thoughts about my sister and how they were better for her being in their life. Today I love my sister with all my heart and will always be grateful for all that she does. My respect and love for her sometimes can be intense when you consider I'm not an emotional type of person. I know if I ever was to need her she'd come running to my side.

The word cancer is tantamount to me and it only

brings back painful memories of both my sister and father. I understand that to fight the disease you must have a strong support structure and have a strong belief in God. I often pray that if I'm ever faced with such a disease I could only have ¼ of my sister's strength and I'll persevere. I have earned a profound respect for the disease that takes so many from this world; when I hear of someone being diagnosed with cancer it brings a tear to my eyes just knowing the battle they will face.

From Keith (Brother; stem cell donor):

The most alarming moment for me was just hearing the words, "your sister has cancer." I thought, "wow double whammy first dad now Regina." Once Regina gathered the info and facts about everything going on , her strong faith and belief in God; not accepting defeat all played a part in her defeating cancer.

I was the most supportive when all the cards where on the table, after diagnosis, fate would have it that I would be part of the solution. ALL OF THE NEEDLES.

Our relationship I guess like all big sister little brother relationships play out she was a bully. She still is a bully just nicer. We love each other and that will never change.

This experience taught me that cancer does not hear, taste, see, feel nor discriminate. The fact that one is diagnosed with cancer does not mean it is the end; in fact it's just the beginning. The beginning of a long journey

From Sharon (Sister):

The initial diagnosis was the scariest for me. I recall getting the news from momma. Keith and I left Starkville and drove to Savannah to visit her. It was difficult to swallow the news given the fact that Daddy was also diagnosed. It takes a determined person to beat this disease. She has the drive to be there for her family along with faith in God. She placed her life in his hands and not the physicians treating her.

We are sisters who don't always agree on things and make it known to one another, however, nothing and no one would ever change the fact that whatever she needs I will be there no matter what! I tried to help the most by taking trips to Starkville to be with momma as she cared for Jeremiah and Devida while Regina and David were in Texas.

Regina is truly a woman of God and a giver. So often she places others' needs ahead of hers and I admire her for that! I appreciate her honesty! I have learned that it is necessary to prepare yourself mind, body and spirit to be able to deal with the disease and everything that comes with the diagnosis. This disease has a tremendous effect on immediate and extended family. I feel you must be strong in your faith and ensure the world around you exhibits positive energy!!!

From friend Janet Lee:

The major concern of course is that Regina would pass. In the interim, I was concerned with her mental and spiritual well-being. Unfortunately, I had moved to another city and could no longer see her as often as I would have liked, so the distance heightened my concerns. There are a few factors that helped Regina get through this ordeal. Regina was born with spunk. Her tenacity is one of her greatest assets. She's a natural fighter which proved to be very helpful in her battle with cancer. She was determined not to be outdone. Actually, I can think of two times where I had to be supportive to my friend. She went to Emory Hospital to get a second opinion. She stayed with me since I lived in Stone Mountain, GA. Her visit was quite disappointing. Not only was the message negative, but it was conveyed in a dismissive tone. This was definitely not what she and David expected.

Although, she left to go back home a little discouraged, I believe the outrage of how she had been treated actually rejuvenated her more than the discouragement and she got her second wind.

I believe we both think of one another as sisters. The only thing that we don't share is familial blood and genes. Our friendship began because of our sons' friendship. Nick (my son) and Jeremiah (Regina's son) were best friends. My husband and I even became

Jeremiah's godparents. Through the years, our friendship quickly blossomed into sisterhood. We share our most intimate thoughts without the worry of being judged or receiving ridicule. Like sisters ought to, we get on one another's nerves, but like sisters ought to, we love one another unconditionally. The biggest lesson that I have learned is the power that your mind and attitude have over the disease. This lesson of power was epitomized for me when I saw her father pass so quickly, yet she is not only still here, but still in remission. God has a plan for her! I also learned that just because you have a reputation of being a great hospital like Emory Hospital, it is important to seek out the experts that specialize in your specific type of cancer.

Medical Terminology

Aspirate is the removal of bone marrow from a donor's iliac crests also known as hip bones (removal by suction of a fluid from a body cavity using a needle)
Biopsy is the medical removal of tissue from a living subject to determine the presence or extent of a disease
Bellicose means aggressive or ready to fight

Bone Marrow is a spongy tissue found in the center of bones; the source of stem cells which evolve into the three kinds of blood cells in the body: red blood cells, white blood cells, and platelets.

Chemotherapy is a combination of drugs that works by destroying rapidly dividing cells.

Catheter is a device which is a thin tube made from medical grade materials inserted into the body to perform surgical procedures. It has a broad range of functions such as allowing drainage, administration of fluids or gases, access by surgical instruments, and also performs wide variety of other tasks depending on the type of catheter. Catheters can be inserted into a body cavity, duct, or vessel.
Immunoglobulin is an antibody produced by cells that is used by the immune system to identify and neutralize foreign objects such as bacteria and viruses.

Oncologist is a specialist who deals with the branch of medicine that focuses on tumors, including the study of their development, diagnosis, treatment, and prevention.

Platelet is a small disk shaped cell fragment which circulates blood and is involved in hemostasis that leads to the formation of blood clots. If the number of platelets if too low, excessive bleeding can occur. However, if the count is too high, blood clots can form which may obstruct blood vessels and result in other events including blockage of blood vessels to other parts of the body (such as extremities of the arms or legs).

Prednisone is a synthetic drug that is particularly effective as an immunosuppressant drug. It is used to treat certain inflammatory diseases and at higher doses some types of cancer, but has significant adverse effects because it suppresses the immune system and leaves patients more susceptible to infections.

Stem cell transplant is a procedure that replaces a person's faulty stem cells with healthy ones. Stem cells are found in bone marrow. The recipient's immune system is usually destroyed with radiation or chemotherapy before the transplantation

(Artwork by Craig Thompson Jr, 2014)

Craig Jr. created this original piece of artwork which captured the essence of Regina's journey. It portrays the love and support received from immediate family, extended family, friends and medical staff. The hands holding the globe represent how everyone reached out to support us. It is also an example of how the support of loved ones collectively held our world up and together as Jeremiah, Devida, and myself did all we could to be strong for Regina.

The image of Regina dancing on top of the world speaks volumes; although the journey was difficult, her decision to open her heart and welcome people into her world allowed Regina to receive the physical and spiritual support which enabled her to conquer the cancer diagnoses.It is interesting to see how Craig Jr.; being 11 years old at the time, comprehended the situation enough to illustrate a picture so beautifully.

It illustrates how he witness people from all walks of life extend themselves to Regina and our family.
And as I look at his picture I am hopeful that others are able to see what I see now from the eyes of a then 11 year old, the important role family can play in coming to your love ones side when they need you the most. Please remember that you have to be open to allowing people into your personal struggles to receive their love and support. Also know that the world is open and willing to extend a helping hand to others we just need to humble ourselves and ask.

About the Author & Survivor

Regina Thompson describes herself as a woman who at a point in time felt the need to be in control of everything. She aspired to be perfect; the perfect wife and mother. Fortunately, her life's trials and tribulations have helped her to appreciate and treasure all the things life has to offer. In other words, she has taken time to stop and smell the roses. Most people compliment her on her ability to remain calm in stressful situations. She embraces challenges and actively looks for the silver lining in every situation. This way of looking at things she believes has proven to be beneficial in her growth as a woman. She however refers to herself as a caring, devoted, wife, mother, daughter, sister and friend. Mrs. Thompson was raised on a farm in Starkville, Mississippi. She has five brothers and sisters whom she shared an awesome childhood with while enjoying 100 acres of freedom on her family land which was inherited by her father and mother. She practically lived in the woods, venturing far out and always finding her way home; she continues to love outdoors because she believes this is when you can see God's work best.

Similar to the late Langston Hughes, "Life for me ain't been no crystal stair"; for two time cancer survivor, Regina Thompson, either. After surviving two bouts with cancer Mrs. Thompson is determined to share her story with people all over the world. She believes that cancer does not have to be the end of your life; and in fact talking and journaling continues to serve as therapy for her. In 1995, Mrs. Thompson faced her first onset of cancer. After being told the cancer symptoms were menopause and several other theories, she soon learned the harsh reality. Unknowledgeable with how to handle the situation Mrs. Thompson began to journal diligently.

After Mrs. Thompson's second triumphant win over cancer in 1997 she decided to pursue her degree in psychology at Armstrong Atlantic State University in Savannah, Georgia. Her primary focus was to understand why people are prone to certain diseases. She began to understand the fundamentals which mostly connected to stress levels. This has served as a proclamation to Mrs. Thompson, that every endeavor will be complimented by talking and journaling more, leading to less internalization.

Today Mrs. Thompson is well and practicing social work in Savannah Georgia. She remains dedicated to helping others understand cancer. In her own words Mrs. Thompson refers to cancer as a "GIFT".

About the Editor

Aminata Traore-Morris is a native of Boston, Massachusetts, but claims Savannah as home. She is a graduate of Lynchburg College and Florida Agricultural & Mechanical University where she studied French, Communications, and Educational Leadership. She loves to travel and has explored places ranging from Dubai, Barbados, France and Senegal, West Africa which is where her father is from. Mrs. Morris aspires to be a communications consultant and provide services such as editing, speech writing, and image consulting and coaching. She is also exploring publishing children's picture books in the near future. She lives in Atlanta with her husband and son. Mrs. Morris can be reached traore.ami77@gmail.com.

About the Artist:

Meekayll Boyd is a 22 year old charcoal artist born and raised in Chicago, IL, until a turn of events led him to the small town of Starkville, Mississippi. Meekayll met a fantastic high school art teacher by the name of Andrew Lark whose sole purpose was to bring out the best abilities of his students. This is where his journey in art truly began. With countless amount of hours honing his skills in charcoal drawings he was finally able to develop a style and technique within art that continues to improve with each work of art created. He dreams that through his artwork he may help others. The meticulous nature of his work and process is grounded in realistic renderings, and his subject matter ranges from portraits and still life to conceptual.

In 2010, Meekayll placed third in the Mississippi State Congressional Art competition. In 2012, he was published in the book Art Takes Times Square. He has also recently been voted to have his work displayed on Taxi-E in The Netherlands by newmasterartist.com. Furthermore Meekayll was accepted as RAW Artist in

2013, an organization that chooses a select group of artists nationally, showcasing their work and talents at a prestigious level. Meekayll's first showcase in 2013 took place in Memphis, TN at Minglewood Hall where he received outstanding feedback from spectators as well from other participating artists and the host of the showcase.

2014 arrived and this began a new journey for Meekayll and his work. He began to expand his name and talents media wise. He was featured on a local news station; WCBI in Mississippi, in a segment called *Mid-Morning with Aundrea Self* speaking about his early years as an artists and his progress today. Meekayl can be reach via his website at www.4evadesigns.com.

Acknowledgements

I want to give recognition to God, for never leaving me on this journey called life, for accepting me back when I got lost along the way and for strategically placing his earth angels, my supports all around me to help during this time. I want to dedicate this book to the memory of my dad, (the late Melvin Thompson) and my Auntie (the late Mary Eliza Thompson). To my mom Joann Thompson, who taught me unconditional love, my personal prayer warrior and my best friend. I love you for all you have done and all you continue to do for me and my family. To my brothers, Calvin (my platelet donor), Craig, Keith (my stem cell donor), Metric and sister Sharon for extending their love by giving me the gift of being able to choose who would be my stem cell donor and platelet donor. I want to extend my deep appreciation for giving me the gift of having a chance at life again. To my children, Jeremiah and Devida, who unknowingly played a pivotal role in the reason I fought so hard to remain a part of their lives today. But most importantly to my husband David, who honored the marriage vows we took before God, ("for better or for worse, in sickness and in health"). I am so blessed to have a man who was and still is willing to be there for me no matter what the circumstances. David also thank you for encouraging me to share my story with others. Love you honey. Thank you Aminata for assisting me with this book process and believing in the project.

www.ingramcontent.com/pod-product-compliance
Lightning Source LLC
La Vergne TN
LVHW052026080426
835513LV00018B/2183